The Twelve Steps for Christians

The Twelve Steps for Christians

REVISED EDITION

Based on Biblical Teachings

. . .

Friends in Recovery

RPI Publishing, Inc.

Published by
RPI Publishing, Inc.
59 Old El Pueblo, Suite E
Scotts Valley, CA 95066
(800) 873-8384

Library of Congress Cataloging-in-Publication Data
The Twelve Steps for Christians: based on biblical teachings /
     Friends in Recovery. — Rev. ed.
p.   cm.
Rev. ed. of: The Twelve steps for Christians from addictive and
other dysfunctional families. c1988.
ISBN 0-941405-57-5 (pbk.)
1. Adult children of narcotic addicts—Religious life. 2. Adult child abuse
victims—Religious life. 3. Adult children of dysfunctional families—Religious
life. 4. Twelve-step programs—Religious aspects—Christians. I. Friends in
Recovery.   II. Title: Twelve Steps for Christians from addictive and other
dysfunctional families.
BV4596.A28T84   1994
248.8'6—dc20.   93-49889
                                                                  CIP

Scripture taken from the Holy Bible, New International Version. Copyright © 1973, 1978, 1984 by International Bible Society. Used by permission of Zondervan Bible Publishers.

The Twelve Steps are reprinted with permission of Alcoholics Anonymous World Services, Inc. Permission to reprint and adapt the Twelve Steps does not mean that AA has reviewed or approved the contents of this publication, nor that AA agrees with the views expressed herein. AA is a program of recovery from alcoholism only—use of the Twelve Steps in connection with programs and activities which are patterned after AA, but which address other problems, does not imply otherwise.

For the purposes of this book, the word "alcohol" in Step One has been changed to read "the effects of our separation from God," and the word "alcoholics" in Step Twelve has been changed to read "others."

Printed in the United States of America

Revised Edition

In memory of Richard, Edward, and others
whose lives were a struggle with addiction,
and who never discovered a
spiritual path to recovery.

For nearly fifty years God has used the healing
power of the Twelve Steps to restore the lives of
countless individuals. He has conveyed this healing
message through people who know what it is
to be broken by life and mended by God.
We dedicate this book to all those
who have found healing through
this spiritual program and who continue
to choose to share their experience,
strength, and hope with those yet searching.

A part of the proceeds from the sale of this book
go to support the work of recovery ministry.

TABLE OF CONTENTS

IMPORTANT INFORMATION

This book is designed to provide information regarding the subject matter covered. It is provided with the understanding that the publisher and authors are not engaged in rendering individualized professional services.

Appendix One contains a suggested meeting format for group study and includes review questions for each step.

Appendix Two contains information about RPI Publishing, Inc.

Appendix Three contains Self-Help Resources.

THE TWELVE STEPS OF
ALCOHOLICS ANONYMOUS

1. We admitted we were powerless over alcohol—that our lives had become unmanageable.
2. Came to believe that a Power greater than ourselves could restore us to sanity.
3. Made a decision to turn our will and our lives over to the care of God *as we understood Him.*
4. Made a searching and fearless moral inventory of ourselves.
5. Admitted to God, to ourselves, and to another human being the exact nature of our wrongs.
6. Were entirely ready to have God remove all these defects of character.
7. Humbly asked Him to remove our shortcomings.
8. Made a list of all persons we had harmed, and became willing to make amends to them all.
9. Made direct amends to such people wherever possible, except when to do so would injure them or others.
10. Continued to take personal inventory and when we were wrong promptly admitted it.
11. Sought through prayer and meditation to improve our conscious contact with God, *as we understood Him,* praying only for knowledge of His will for us and the power to carry that out.
12. Having had a spiritual awakening as the result of these steps, we tried to carry this message to alcoholics, and to practice these principles in all our affairs.

THE TWELVE STEPS
AND RELATED SCRIPTURE

STEP ONE

We admitted we were powerless over the effects
of our separation from God—that our lives
had become unmanageable.

• • •

*I know nothing good lives in me, that is, in my sinful
nature. For I have the desire to do what is good,
but I cannot carry it out.* (ROM. 7:18)

STEP TWO

Came to believe that a power greater than
ourselves could restore us to sanity.

• • •

*For it is God who works in you to will and to act
according to his good purpose.* (PHIL. 2:13)

STEP THREE

Made a decision to turn our will and our lives over
to the care of God *as we understood Him.*

• • •

*Therefore, I urge you, brothers, in view of God's mercy,
to offer your bodies as living sacrifices, holy
and pleasing to God—which is your
spiritual worship.* (ROM. 12:1)

STEP FOUR

Made a searching and fearless
moral inventory of ourselves.

• • •

*Let us examine our ways and test them, and let
us return to the Lord.* (LAM. 3:40)

STEP FIVE

Admitted to God, to ourselves, and to another human
being the exact nature of our wrongs.

• • •

*Therefore confess your sins to each other
and pray for each other so that you
may be healed.* (JAMES 5:16A)

STEP SIX

Were entirely ready to have God remove
all these defects of character.

• • •

*Humble yourselves before the Lord, and he
will lift you up.* (JAMES 4:10)

STEP SEVEN

Humbly asked Him to remove our shortcomings.

• • •

*If we confess our sins, he is faithful and just and
will forgive us our sins and purify us from
all unrighteousness.* (1 JOHN 1:9)

STEP EIGHT

Made a list of all persons we had harmed and became
willing to make amends to them all.

• • •

*Do to others as you would have
them do to you.* (LUKE 6:31)

STEP NINE

Made direct amends to such people wherever possible,
except when to do so would injure them or others.

• • •

*Therefore, if you are offering your gift at the altar and
there remember that your brother has something
against you, leave your gift there in front of the altar. First go
and be reconciled to your brother; then come
and offer your gift.* (MATT. 5:23–24)

STEP TEN

Continued to take personal inventory, and when we
were wrong, promptly admitted it.

• • •

*So, if you think you are standing firm, be careful
that you don't fall.* (1 COR. 10:12)

STEP ELEVEN

Sought through prayer and meditation to improve our
conscious contact with God *as we understood Him,*
praying only for knowledge of His will for us
and the power to carry that out.

• • •

Let the word of Christ dwell in
you richly. (COL. 3:16A)

STEP TWELVE

Having had a spiritual awakening as the result of these steps, we tried to carry this message to others, and to practice these principles in all our affairs.

• • •

Brothers, if someone is caught in a sin, you who
are spiritual should restore him gently. But
watch yourself, or you also may
be tempted. (GAL. 6:1)

THE TWELVE STEPS AND SPIRITUAL DISCIPLINES

Goal	Step	Discipline
Peace with God	**Step One** is about recognizing our brokenness	Submission
	Step Two is about the birth of faith in us	Conversion
	Step Three involves a decision to let God be in charge of our lives.	
Peace with Ourselves	**Step Four** involves self-examination	Confession
	Step Five is the discipline of confession	
	Step Six is an inner tranformation sometimes called repentance	Repentance
	Step Seven involves the transformation or purification of our character	
Peace with Others	**Step Eight** involves examining our relationships and preparing ourselves to make amends	Amends
	Step Nine is the discipline of making amends	
	Step Ten is about maintaining progress in recovery	Maintenance
Keeping the Peace	**Step Eleven** involves the spiritual disciplines of prayer and meditation	Prayer
	Step Twelve is about ministry	Repentance

CHRISTIAN ROOTS OF
THE TWELVE STEPS

Alcoholics Anonymous began on June 10, 1935, co-founded by William Griffith Wilson (Bill W.) and Dr. Robert Holbrook Smith (Dr. Bob). Wilson conceived the idea of Alcoholics Anonymous while he was hospitalized for excessive drinking in December of 1934. During his hospital stay, Wilson had a spiritual experience that removed his desire to drink. In the following months, he tried to persuade other alcoholics to stop drinking just as he had. Wilson found his first "convert" in Smith, who was willing to follow Wilson's method to find freedom from alcoholism. Four years later, Wilson and Smith published the book, *Alcoholics Anonymous*, which contains the Twelve Steps and a spiritually based program of recovery for alcoholism.

THE OXFORD GROUP

Various sources influenced the formulation of AA's program, as developed and recorded by Wilson. Of these, the British-born Oxford Group movement and its American leader, Episcopal clergyman Samuel Moor Shoemaker, Jr., contributed most significantly to the Christian basis of Alcoholics Anonymous. Both Wilson and Smith attended the Oxford Group meetings and based much of the AA program on this framework.

In the 1920s and 1930s, the Oxford Group movement became a revolutionary answer to antireligious reaction following World War I. Aiming to rekindle living faith in a church gone stale with institutionalism, the Oxford Group declared itself an "organism" rather than an "organization."

Group members met in homes and hotels, mingling religion with meals. Despite its freedom from institutional ties, the movement was distinctly ecclesiastical and looked to the church as its authority.

Dr. Frank N. D. Buchman, a Lutheran pastor, is often cited as leader of the Oxford movement. Yet, if one were to ask an Oxford Group follower, "Who is your leader?" the reply might be, "The Holy Spirit." So confidently did the group believe in the guidance of the Spirit that it had no organized board of officers, but relied instead on "God control" through men and women who had fully "surrendered" to God's will. Buchman emphasized the need to surrender to God for forgiveness and guidance and to confess one's sins to God and others. Oxford Group followers learned to make restitution for wrongs done and to witness about their changed lives in order to help change others.

The Oxford Group's teachings rested on the following six basic assumptions:

1. Human beings are sinners.
2. Human beings can be changed.
3. Confession is a prerequisite to change.
4. The changed soul has direct access to God.
5. The age of miracles has returned.
6. Those who have been changed are to change others.[1]

In addition, Wilson incorporated into AA's philosophy the Oxford Group's five procedures, which were:

1. Giving to God.
2. Listening to God's direction.
3. Checking guidance.

[1] Cantril, Hadley, *The Psychology of Social Movements* (Huntington, NY: Robert E. Kruger, 1941), pp. 147–148.

4. Restitution.
5. Sharing, both confession and witness.[2]

EVOLUTION OF THE TWELVE STEPS

While trying to attract more followers to sobriety from 1935–1937, Smith and Wilson attended Oxford Group meetings in New York led by Samuel Moor Shoemaker, Jr. "It was from Sam Shoemaker that we absorbed most of the Twelve Steps of Alcoholics Anonymous, steps that express the heart of A.A.'s way of life," Wilson later recalled. "The early A.A. got its ideas of self-examination, acknowledgement of character defects, restitution for harm done, and working with others straight from the Oxford Group and directly from Sam Shoemaker, their former leader in America, and from nowhere else."[3]

---

[2] Kurtz, Ernest, *Not God: A History of Alcoholics Anonymous* (Center City, MN: Hazelden Educational Materials, 1979) pp. 48–49.
[3] *Alcoholics Anonymous Comes of Age* (New York: Alcoholics Anonymous World Services, Inc., 1957), p. 199.

PREFACE

Those who participated in the writing and review of this material are recovering Christian lay people and clergy. Their belief is that Scripture and the Twelve Steps are important healing tools. They believe that if we regularly apply these tools to our lives, we open ourselves to God's healing love and grace. Their intention is to carry the message of the Twelve Steps and Christ's love to all hurting people.

This revised edition reflects the spiritual and emotional growth of its contributors. It is also an expression of their commitment to work their individual programs and apply the principles of the Twelve Steps to their daily lives. The foundation of each contributor's recovery process is his or her relationship with a loving Higher Power, God, as personalized in Jesus Christ.

A central theme and assumption of this work is that healing is possible. To some degree or another, everyone can experience freedom from the damaging effects of a less-than-nurturing environment. As our wounds heal, we become functional members of the community.

Working the Twelve Steps helps us reclaim our birthright as children of a compassionate God. We were created in his image and have the gift of free will. The journey we are about to begin is intended to awaken us to God's grace and give us an opportunity to experience peaceful and productive living. Feelings of unworthiness, anxiety, and inferiority diminish and are replaced by spiritual strength and virtues. Focusing on our new relationship with God transforms our obsessive need for other people's approval.

Our attention is, instead, captivated by the promise of new life in Christ.

The Twelve Traditions of Alcoholics Anonymous stress personal anonymity as a vital element of one's recovery. As "Friends in Recovery," we have chosen to remain anonymous to pursue our own personal growth. We understand the importance of facing ourselves honestly and placing our confidence in the person of Jesus Christ. We offer these materials, not as an end in themselves, but as a means to developing a healthy relationship with God, with others, and with oneself.

INTRODUCTION TO
REVISED EDITION

The revisions in this book are the result of the authors' continued growth and recommendations received from individuals using the book. It is through their willingness to share their experience of utilizing the material that these changes are possible. Improvements in the text are a result of feedback from groups using this book.

The Twelve Steps for Christians is a personal guide to understanding the spiritual power of the Twelve Steps from a Christian perspective. This material is primarily for adults whose childhoods were negatively affected by a less-than-nurturing environment. This environment often resulted when the adults responsible for care were influenced by substance abuse, emotional problems, or compulsive behaviors. The Twelve Steps offer a way to grow beyond the harmful effects of a troubled home environment. Since the founding of Alcoholics Anonymous in 1935, the Twelve Steps have become a way for millions of people to change the course of their lives.

Twelve-Step recovery is not a program sponsored by any religious group or entity. However, people using this program find it in harmony with their own spiritual beliefs. It has no official religious affiliation. It is, however, a program that helps us to rediscover and deepen the spiritual part of ourselves. We also realize through working the Twelve Steps that our spirituality is important. We learn to live our lives according to the guidance of God, our Higher Power. We realize that the void or despair we feel is the result of our ignoring or rejecting our relationship with our Lord, Jesus Christ.

The foundation for this book is the Twelve-Step process. This process has helped countless individuals recover from many forms of addictive, compulsive, or obsessive behavior. This book is a tool for developing one's personal journey toward recovery. It brings together the tested wisdom of Bible truths and the proven effectiveness of Twelve-Step principles. The material encourages self-understanding and emphasizes the unchanging love of God for all humanity.

The Twelve Steps for Christians contains scriptural passages that illustrate the harmony between the practice of Christianity and the working of the Twelve Steps. The use of Scripture provides an understanding of the Twelve Steps within a biblical context. When used as intended, the steps are a profoundly powerful process for allowing God to heal damaged emotions. This book is a spiritual tool that helps us regain balance and order, and leads us to improved health and increased happiness through a renewed relationship with God.

As Christians we believe that God reveals much of his plan for each of us in the Holy Scriptures. Both mature Christians and those who are just being awakened to a personal relationship with Christ can find tremendous value in the Twelve Steps. By regularly applying them to the events of one's life, the steps become a means for enriching one's relationship with God. The steps are especially powerful when used together with the regular Christian practices of prayer, meditation, and Bible study. We will discover the unique ways in which the Holy Scriptures support and expand our understanding of the steps.

The Twelve-Step process of recovery is a spiritual journey. It takes us from a life where we experience confusion and grief to a place of peace and serenity—one day at a time. Many changes can and will come over us, but they won't happen all at once. The process takes time and patience.

God, in his time, instills in us the strength of character that only comes from a healthy relationship with him.

We may have many self-defeating habits or behaviors that need correcting. When looking at our inappropriate methods of relating to others, it is important to remember the ways in which these patterns began. Because of the chaotic conditions of our childhood, we developed behaviors that now sabotage and assault the successful management of our lives as adults. Having grown up in emotionally repressive families, we became accustomed to denying our pain and discomfort. During our early years, most of us found it necessary to shut down our feelings and keep everything locked inside. We learned in childhood that expressing our own wants and needs caused rejection. This rejection stimulated the onset of intense feelings of inadequacy and shame.

In our present environments, we may have trouble freely expressing pain, fear, anger, or need. We repress our true feelings because we continue to view our environment the same as we did in childhood. When we openly express our needs, we risk rejection. In order to avoid rejection, many of us compensate for our repressed feelings by doing things to extremes. Our behavior may include preoccupation with relationships, our church, and our job. Or we may cover our true feelings through overwork, overeating, or abuse of mood-altering substances such as drugs and alcohol.

The healing process begins when we look honestly at ourselves. We see the chaotic conditions of our lives as a result of not being prepared for adult relationships and responsibilities. God has given us free will. We can choose several ways of relating to the people and events in our lives. It is important to set aside some of our negative childhood messages and begin the work of learning new behaviors that will better serve us.

Some of us were taught to believe that, if we are Christians, our lives will "automatically" be in order, and we will experience peace and serenity. Yet many Christians know their lives are in turmoil despite their intense devotion to religion. Time, patience, and commitment to God's principles and ways are required to change. And our Christian experience doesn't magically erase the pain or consequences of the past. Instead, our faith empowers us to live life according to God's will.

For Christians who suffer from an addictive disease or who are the product of a family with addictive traits, the Church's message can sometimes be perceived as shaming. This can keep a person from seeking recovery. There is rarely confusion, however, when the Church's message is honesty. The Bible modeled this honesty by documenting the strengths and weaknesses of God's people. Unfortunately, for some, to admit to imperfection might mean that we are not good Christians. In reality, to admit to imperfection means *we need God,* and that's OK. True recovery begins as we work the spiritual principles embodied in the Twelve Steps. And true recovery is most easily accomplished when we acknowledge our need for help, comfort, and courage to face our problems.

Working the steps with God's help enables us to acknowledge much of our negative or repressed nature. This process is similar to sunlight and shadow. When we stand in the sunlight, we see that we cast a shadow. In the same way, as we begin to work the steps and measure ourselves by God's standards and principles, we see our need. But standing before the Lord and seeking his healing grace does not automatically relieve us of the consequences of our past behavior. We do find, however, that by asking God for help in facing our old behaviors, we are able to begin the work of change and healing.

Diligently seeking God's will for us and seriously embracing the material in this book enables us to reexamine our relationship with God. This process helps us discover new ways in which the Holy Spirit empowers our daily lives. We learn to look fearlessly at our "shadow"—that part of us that has been ignored for so long. With the help of God's grace we experience changes in our unwanted behaviors such as people pleasing, repressed anger, obsessive thinking, or inappropriate sexual behavior. Through our relationship with Christ we are able to redefine the limits we set for ourselves, and we discover that "all things are possible" for those who love God.

Thought: God's judgment: we get what we deserve.
God's mercy: we don't get what we deserve.
God's grace: we get more than we deserve.
God doesn't have any problems, only plans.

With God's power, the Twelve-Step program becomes a tool to relieve our suffering, fill our emptiness, and help us extend God's presence in our lives. This releases energy, love, and joy that are new to us. It is a program that we follow at our own pace, in our own way. We walk this journey one step at a time, with God's help and with the support of others in the program. All we need is an open mind. Much of the work is done by God's Spirit working through us. If we work the steps faithfully, we notice improvements in ourselves: our awareness, our sensitivity, our ability to love and be free. Our spiritual and emotional growth may surprise us.

GOD BLESS YOU.

STARTING YOUR
SPIRITUAL PILGRIMAGE

This book provides a practical way to use the Twelve Steps as a recovery tool, and to fully integrate the steps as an ongoing part of our spiritual pilgrimage. The book uses biblical insight to help us identify and deal with issues that are interfering with our lives. Working through these issues requires that we rely on the dynamics of God's word and the Twelve Steps. If we approach this work seriously, we will experience recovery that nurtures physical, emotional, and spiritual well-being.

Trust in God's guidance and support is necessary. In this program, it is important to realize that God wants us to be returned to wholeness. He gives us the courage to work, to struggle, and to succeed. God also gives us the comfort we need to give him control of our lives and to surrender to the Twelve-Step process.

If you are new to the Twelve Steps, it is important to use other resources to help identify more specific issues that pertain to you. Many anonymous Twelve-Step programs have meetings that are focused on issues of relationships, food, sex, alcohol, drugs, etc. Taking part in groups such as Adult Children of Alcoholics, Co-Dependents Anonymous, or Al-Anon broadens your understanding of recovery issues and exposes you to others who share similar problems. You learn more about your own issues and have a sounding board for matters that may arise in your life. We encourage you to read additional material relating to the issues that are problems for you. This increases your awareness and enhances your ability to participate in the process. The Self-Help Resources listed in Appendix Three will help you identify an appropriate program for you. Other resources are also available through your library or in the telephone directory under "social service organizations" or "crisis intervention."

The Twelve Steps are a spiritual pilgrimage. They can be used as a way out of self-destructive behavior, as a laboratory in which to learn new behavior, and as a way to establish a closer relationship with God. When the steps are used in conjunction with support groups, they provide an opportunity to experience feelings, talk openly with others, enjoy life one day at a time, and develop healthy relationships. Meeting together in a group can be a powerful and transforming process. Loneliness diminishes as friendships among group members develop. Individuals can learn to be close to others by giving as well as receiving comfort and support. Communication outside the meeting is a vital element in the recovery process. Use the telephone and other ways to socialize and support one another outside the regular meeting time.

Relationships formed in support groups are a source of many benefits and rewards. The experience of being in a support group creates an atmosphere in which healthy family-type communications can develop. It is a safe environment where trust can be learned. The groups provide an arena for quality sharing in which family secrets no longer need to be hidden, and the process of loving self-parenting can begin.

Wherever possible, share your insights with someone you trust. Communicating your discoveries to a trusted person can work miracles in your recovery journey. You will have an opportunity to share with others in your support group who can provide support and encouragement. As you share with others and build new relationships during this journey, be aware that they are not there to give advice or to fix you. The healing results from developing a relationship with your Higher Power.

Due to our early exposure to negative behavior, many inappropriate behaviors may appear normal to us (e.g., resentment, greed, sexual abuse, dishonesty, gluttony, envy, laziness). Negative feelings may also seem normal (e.g., self-pity, sadness, insecurity, worry, fear of rejection, fear of abandonment). As we progress through the steps, this habit of seeing negative feelings or behavior as normal will change. We will experience growth in all areas by an increased sense of self-worth and self-esteem. Therefore, honest feelings and thoughts need to be appreciated and encouraged. This makes it possible to air elements of discouragement or distress before they hinder the group's progress.

Don't be discouraged if Steps One, Two, and Three seem overwhelming to you—this is a common reaction for persons who are new to the steps. A proper understanding and grasp of these first three steps form the foundation for working the program. Allow sufficient time to digest these steps. This may take some time. Be patient with yourself. Consider the contents and reflect on the meaning of each step. Impatience can seriously impair your effectiveness.

It is likely you will go through these steps more than once. The program is a lifelong process to be used regularly, in part or in whole. At some point you could consider participating in a group that uses *The Twelve Steps—A Spiritual Journey*, a workbook that applies questions and exercises to the materials in this book. This book should not be your only involvement. It is just one part of working the Twelve Steps.

The Twelve-Step material used in this book is a framework upon which our own life experiences can be reviewed with love and courage. We realize we have reached this point knowing very little about ourselves. As we develop a deeper relationship with God, more will be revealed to us. Slowly we will be given the strength to put the past behind us and build a new life. The depth of our relationship with God will be increased as our knowledge of him increases (Psalm 119). Our lives can become less complicated if we work the steps regularly and continue to improve our relationship with God, our Higher Power. When we do this, our lives are blessed with God's ongoing gift of peace and serenity (John 14:27).

Give freely of yourself and join us. We shall be with you in the fellowship of God's Holy Spirit.

WORKING WITH A RECOVERY PARTNER

The concern, support, and input of others is essential to the recovery process. One way to ensure this support is through working with a recovery partner. Ecclesiastes 4:9–12 conveys the principle of Christ-centered partnership: *"Two are better than one, because they have a good return for their work. If one falls down, his friend can help him up. But pity the man who falls and has no one to help him up! ...Though one may be overpowered, two can defend themselves. A cord of three strands is not quickly broken."*

A "recovery partner" is someone who will be there for us when the support group is not, someone who can be called between meetings, and who can be confided in and trusted. A recovery partner can be relied upon for prayer and can help us recognize how denial keeps us from discovering the truth about ourselves. Working with a recovery partner makes it easier to identify our fears and resentments, as well as our self-defeating and addictive behavior.

Sharing with a recovery partner offers us an opportunity to have a one-on-one relationship without the distractions found when groups meet together. For individuals who have felt betrayed in the past, this is an opportunity to develop mutual trust by communicating privately with a recovery partner. We can reveal ourselves to another person without feeling intimidated by others in a group setting. This dynamic can cause a breakthrough in learning to trust in someone and in being willing to share openly about their life experiences.

CHOOSING A RECOVERY PARTNER

A recovery partner is similar to a mentor or sponsor. This person can be a role model for learning how to enjoy a better quality of life through the love of God and the wisdom of the program. It is important to choose someone who displays qualities you value and respect. These qualities can include:

- Belief in the Christian faith and a willingness to share his or her walk with God.

- Sincerity and honesty in sharing personal stories of recovery and how the Twelve Steps work in his or her life.

- Willingness to provide support and encouragement by listening and giving honest feedback without trying to force change.

- Ability to confront difficult issues and ask for accountability in keeping commitments.

- Openness of communication in all matters, even when discussing sensitive issues such as sexual abuse, violence, or other severe trauma-inducing subjects.

When choosing a recovery partner, it is advisable to select an individual who:

- Shares common interests and experiences and displays positive results in recovery.

- Understands and identifies with addictive, compulsive, or obsessive behavior.

- Has patience and compassion and is willing to listen attentively and offer suggestions without giving advice.

- Is available to spend time together when it is necessary.

- Is the same sex and can relate to personal issues in a nonthreatening way.

Some questions and expectations that arise when choosing a recovery partner are:

- **What about the fear of rejection?** The process of dealing with fear of rejection can occur when asking someone to be a recovery partner. Because the program encourages rigorous honesty, we should begin by honestly telling the other person about any discomfort we feel when seeking a recovery partnership. We should offer the other person freedom of choice in the decision, and then detach from the outcome by trusting that God's will prevails.

- **What happens when you are asked to be a partner and don't want to be?** This program can help us establish boundaries for ourselves. Boundaries include how we spend our time, express our feelings, and enter new relationships. Knowing when to say "Thank you for asking, but that won't work for me" is all a part of setting boundaries. Setting boundaries can be an important step in simplifying our life, and it does not require an explanation.

- **What about ending a recovery partnership?** Ending a recovery-partner relationship is part of learning when to select more appropriate support. It is also a reminder that one person may not meet the needs of the recovery partner forever. Personal growth is a natural part of the process. The outcome may still be a very good friendship.

BENEFITS OF A RECOVERY PARTNER

There are benefits to be gained from working with a recovery partner, including the fulfillment of many biblical admonitions. Below is a list of some of the benefits with related biblical references.

- Partners provide a nonthreatening system of mutual accountability. For example, a partner can agree to call the other for support and prayer in abstaining from a harmful habit.

"Therefore confess your sins to each other and pray for each other so that you may be healed. The prayer of a righteous man is powerful and effective." (JAMES 5:14–16)

• Partners minister to each other's specific areas of need with directed prayer each time they meet. Openly sharing thoughts and feelings helps to clarify needs in problem areas. This contributes to our freedom from the past. The focus is to live honestly in the present with realistic expectations.

"Pray continually; give thanks in all circumstances, for this is God's will for you in Christ Jesus." (1 THESS. 5:17)

• Partners encourage one another to progress from a state of physical, emotional, and spiritual sickness to wholeness of life. It is normal to feel discomfort when unhealthy familiar behaviors are being transformed. Healthy behavior is a result of doing God's will.

"...consider how we may spur one another on toward love and good deeds." (HEB. 10:24)

• Partners aid one another in applying biblical truths to personal and relationship needs. When partners openly share their faults with one another, honesty, trust, and healing occur. This also means we can appropriately quote Scripture to shed light on an experience. It is not appropriate to over-spiritualize and lose the vulnerability of the moment or lose the point of what is shared.

Jesus said, " 'If you hold to my teaching, you are really my disciples. Then you will know the truth, and the truth will set you free.' " (JOHN 8:31–32)

MUTUAL AGREEMENT
BETWEEN RECOVERY PARTNERS

A key part in establishing a relationship with a recovery partner is to agree on how the partners want to interact with one another. The agreement can establish:

- What the expectations are between one another.
- The length of time in which the agreement will be in effect.
- Specified times to evaluate the quality of the relationship.
- An understanding of how the relationship or agreement can be ended.

The agreement encourages the partners to make a sincere effort to:

- Focus on the Twelve Steps as a tool to enhance one's relationship with God and others.

  At times encouragement or confrontation is needed when one has stopped working the steps. If a partner is unavailable or can't answer a question, seek out other Twelve-Step fellow travelers to help in understanding how they use this discipline in their recovery. It is inappropriate to impose personal views on one's recovery partner, particularly regarding one's relationship with God.

- Be available for phone calls or meeting in person.

  A key to success in recovery is making and keeping commitments. Making a commitment to being available may be something new, but it is an important part of the process. Healing and change are easier when someone is available to offer support and encouragement.

- Share my true feelings with my recovery partner.

Rigorous honesty is important when sharing feelings. Healing is supported when partners tell the truth. Feelings require acknowledgment and appropriate expression without their being judged as right or wrong. Selective disclosure when talking about feelings may create doubt between partners.

• Respect confidentiality and refrain from gossip.

This program is built on trust. Fear of gossip may prevent some people from honestly sharing their pain. Healing will be hindered unless there is trust that personal matters between partners will remain confidential.

• Accept discomfort as part of the healing process, and be willing to talk about it.

Some meetings may be painful when memories of certain events or hurtful feelings are recalled. It is important to have a recovery partner available to show compassion and be supportive as we confront painful issues that cause us discomfort. It is best to admit the discomfort and deal with it. A recovery partner can help us face with the issues without reverting to old coping methods.

• Support one another by listening attentively and offering constructive feedback.

Listening attentively and offering feedback enables us to explore options and possible courses of action. This can strengthen one another's ability to make healthy choices that provide good results. Feedback, however, must not be confused with unsolicited advice.

• Refrain from over-spiritualizing or intellectualizing when sharing.

Partners are not spiritual directors to each other nor are they sources of advice in areas more appropriately handled by clergy or professional therapists. Instead, partners share their own experience, strength, and hope with one another. In spiritual matters, recovery partners share how God works in their life without over-spiritualizing or preaching.

- Spend a minimum of 15 minutes each day reading Scripture, praying, and meditating, including prayer for your recovery partner.

Prayer is talking to God, meditation is listening to God. Spending time in prayer and meditation can be a vital part of the recovery process. This is a spiritual program founded upon seeking to know God's will and experiencing His grace.

FINAL THOUGHTS

It is important to be tolerant and accepting of our recovery partner and others. This does not mean condoning addictive behavior slips or the rationalizations that follow. Being able to detach with love means not taking the behavior breakdown as a personal affront that one has somehow failed the recovery partner.

Partners are not responsible for each other. Their responsibility is to listen and respond from their own experience, strength, and hope. Having a trusted person who listens to us is helpful when working through the decision-making process. Having a recovery partner may be a way to experience the unconditional love of God for the first time.

NOTE: Two new books have recently been released by RPI Publishing as companions to *The Twelve Steps for Christians* and *The Twelve Steps—A Spiritual Journey*. The first book, *Meditations for The Twelve Steps—A Spiritual Journey*, is a series of stories and reflections from every-day life using the

Scriptures contained in each step. These devotional thoughts are written from the perspective of someone in the program, and provide a source of experience, strength, and hope. The second book, *Prayers for The Twelve Steps—A Spiritual Journey,* provides the reader with a rich understanding of prayer. It describes the various types of prayer and includes actual prayers written by program members over the years.

COMMON BEHAVIOR CHARACTERISTICS

Adults who were reared in dysfunctional homes share certain common behavior characteristics. This is especially true when their caretakers were chemically dependent or emotionally repressed individuals. The behaviors reveal an underlying structure of disorder that is damaging to those involved. Although the general population displays many of the behaviors, individuals from dysfunctional families tend to have a higher incidence of these characteristics. This exercise is intended to help you identify the areas of your life in which dysfunctional behavior characteristics are present. Examples are given to help you identify some of your thoughts, feelings, and behaviors.

• We have feelings of low self-esteem that cause us to judge ourselves and others without mercy. We cover up or compensate by trying to be perfect, take responsibility for others, control the outcome of unpredictable events, get angry when things don't go our way, or gossip instead of confronting an issue. For example:

  – I am unhappy in a church, and I think everyone at church is fraught with imperfections and problems.

  – I feel out of place at work.

  – I'm inclined to talk about my family and extended family. I often recite all of their faults and shortcomings to others.

  – When I am alone with my own thoughts I tend to criticize myself. Sometimes I feel stupid, inadequate, ugly, or worthless.

- I never really feel accepted, so I overachieve to become noticed.

- I don't feel important. I try to help others and hope they will notice me.

- I feel incompetent at work.

- I gossip and complain about those who make me feel powerless.

• We tend to isolate ourselves and to feel uneasy around other people, especially authority figures. For example:

- I don't draw attention to myself at church. I come late to services, sit in the back, and leave early.

- I like to blend into the scenery at work. I especially don't want the boss to notice me.

- I rely heavily on my answering machine at home using it to "screen calls" even when I'm home.

- I feel uncomfortable in most conversations, especially when the focus is on me.

- When I speak with someone in authority, I have trouble expressing myself.

- Whenever there is a police car behind me, I know that the officer is watching me.

- I isolate myself because it's easier than dealing with others.

• We are approval seekers and will do anything to make people like us. We are extremely loyal even in the face of evidence that suggests loyalty is undeserved. For example:

- I offer to do favors for people even before they ask.

- At work or church I take on more projects than I can possibly handle.

- I worry about what others are thinking and saying about me. When people stop talking as I approach, I assume they're talking about me.

- Although I may not like my boss or friends, I am loyal because I fear being rejected.

- I will brag about my accomplishments, achievements, or good work to receive some appreciation or praise. But when colleagues or friends do show praise I am unable to accept it.

- I find it hard to admit that I came from a dysfunctional home. I feel guilty for admitting that my parents were less than perfect.

• We are intimidated by angry people and personal criticism. This causes us to feel anxious and overly sensitive. For example:

- I find it nearly impossible to listen to a "fire and brimstone" sermon.

- When someone with strong opinions speaks to me, I rarely share my true feelings. Instead, I say what I think the other person wants to hear.

- I sometimes harbor a secret desire to retaliate against the angry and opinionated people who threaten my peace.

- I panic when someone points out a mistake or a problem with my work.

- I assume that a family member or friend is angry or unhappy with me if they express a desire to see me change or grow in a given area.

- When I feel that someone has unfairly criticized me, I dream of ways to retaliate. I go out of my way to prove the other person wrong. I broadcast the unfair treatment, or I look for friends who will agree with me and comfort me.

- We habitually choose to have relationships with emotionally unavailable people with addictive personalities. We are usually less attracted to healthy, caring people. For example:
  - I am in a relationship with someone who seems uncaring. I sense that my problems don't matter.
  - I feel that I am always meeting my spouse's needs, but my spouse never makes an effort to meet my needs.
  - I spend a lot of time wondering what it would be like to be married to somebody else.
  - Life is always a crisis. I wonder what it would be like to live a normal life.
  - Others and not myself seem to set the agenda for my life.
  - I sometimes feel that I deserve to "give in" to temptation, especially after I've suffered and done so much for others.

- We live life as victims and are attracted to other victims in our love and friendship relationships. We confuse love with pity and tend to "love" people we can pity and rescue. For example:
  - I feel that I don't deserve the life I'm living.
  - I seem to get the short end of every stick, and I agree with the saying, "No good deed goes unpunished."
  - I almost feel good about myself when I am doing something for others. However, I've learned from experience that they won't appreciate it.
  - My friends tell me that I am a good listener, but I resent how they lose interest when I share.

- I spend a lot of my time fixing other people's problems.
- My resources and finances are always being used to settle someone else's crisis.
- I rarely do things I want to do when I am with others.

• We are either overly responsible or very irresponsible. We try to solve others' problems or expect others to be responsible for us. This enables us to avoid looking closely at our own behavior. For example:

- I believe it is my job to settle family squabbles.
- I am usually called when family members have a problem.
- No one at my job or church cares as much or works as hard as I do.
- I always accept more work than I can handle.
- When things fail at home or at work, I feel that I have somehow failed.

OR

- I feel that I am too disabled to contribute.
- Others don't understand how sick I really am, and I'm expected to do too much.
- After all I've done, I think that others should leave me alone. I'm just not appreciated or understood.
- I'm just waiting for the right opportunity to become reinvolved in life.
- I'm waiting for God to make positive changes in my life.

• We feel guilty when we stand up for ourselves or act assertively. We give in to others instead of taking care of ourselves. For example:

- After I leave a conversation with a pushy person, I think, "I wish I had said this or that or really spoken my mind."

- After I stand up for myself, I feel guilty and think maybe I was wrong after all.

- Although I disagree with someone, I can't say what I'm really thinking.

- When I feel safe with a close friend or family member, I share all my resentments about the pushy people in my life.

- I feel sick when I'm told that certain people want to see me or talk to me.

- I store a great deal of anger inside instead of releasing it properly. I sometimes scream, slam doors, or break things when no one is around.

• We deny, minimize, or repress our feelings. We have difficulty expressing our feelings and are unaware of the impact this has on our lives. For example:

- There are portions of my childhood that I simply cannot remember.

- I sometimes react with overwhelming panic, anxiety, or fear in certain situations, and I have no idea why.

- I find it hard to get really excited about things. Other people are annoyed when I don't share their excitement.

- I guard against too much of any emotion, fearing that any display of joy might bring some catastrophe.

- My spouse or companion complains that I am not very warm.

- When I start to feel too much anxiety or fear or when I hear the committee in my head, I look for something to distract me or kill the pain.

- We are dependent personalities who are terrified of rejection or abandonment. We tend to stay in jobs or relationships that are harmful to us. Our fears can either stop us from ending hurtful relationships or prevent us from entering healthy, rewarding ones. For example:

  - I hate my job, but I don't quit. My friends and family have advised me to try another kind of work.

  - When someone close to me is silent or emotionally absent, I panic and fear the worst.

  - If my superiors don't seem to recognize my work, I assume that they are displeased and ready to let me go.

  - When I disagree with a friend or companion, I later fear that I have irreparably damaged the relationship. I may even call several times to smooth things over or apologize.

  - I spend time daydreaming about what it would be like to have a different job, spouse, friends, etc.

  - I would love to escape my life for a while, but I'm scared to death that I would have nowhere to go and no one to turn to.

- Denial, isolation, control, and misplaced guilt are symptoms of family dysfunction. Because of these behaviors, we feel hopeless and helpless. For example:

  - I just wish that people would leave me alone.

  - Sometimes I can't wait to go home, close the door, and disconnect from reality.

  - I try to manage my own life, but circumstance and other people are always invading my plan.

  - I work hard to reveal little about myself, or I try to manage what people think of me.

- I don't always tell the whole truth when I talk about myself. I tell people just enough about myself and nothing more.

- I often recall my past mistakes. I even tell myself how stupid I am.

- I don't have much hope that things will change. Good things happen to others, but not me. I seem to be cursed, or something.

• We have difficulty with intimate relationships. We feel insecure and lack trust in others. We don't have clearly defined boundaries and become enmeshed with our partner's needs and emotions. For example:

- I feel that maybe my spouse was trapped into marrying me and that now he/she regrets it.

- When my spouse or companion is depressed or down, I assume that it is my fault. I find it impossible to feel better until he/she does.

- If someone close to me is angry, I immediately feel threatened, even if the anger is toward another person or outside force.

- I can have sex with my spouse, but I sometimes find it difficult to be really close or romantic.

- I often belittle my looks (if only to myself) or doubt my attractiveness.

- I may try to change my spouse or companion's mood by suggesting some pleasurable activity.

• We have difficulty following projects through from beginning to end. For example:

- I finish most projects at the last minute.

- My desk is full of great projects that I *was* excited about but never handled.

- People often ask me "whatever happened to...(some project or hobby)?" I say that something more important came up, but the truth is, I lost interest.

- I have stacks of letters and papers on my desk that are waiting for attention.

- I have at least one room (or more) in my house that I hope no one ever sees.

- I feel guilty when I think of all the time and resources I've wasted on half-baked ideas or schemes.

• We have a strong need to be in control. We overreact to change over which we have no control. For example:

- I want to know what my spouse or children are doing. I may even search their private belongings.

- I have been known to listen in on conversations where I wasn't welcome.

- My children tell me that I am suffocating them. Sometimes they threaten to leave home early or run away.

- If other people work for me, I find it hard to let them express their creativity. I want things done my way.

- I become very angry when an order from a fast-food restaurant is not right.

- When serious things happen that are beyond my control, I panic and take out my frustration on others near me. Or I take control through a flurry of activity.

- When my children have the slightest problem, I can't rest until I have done everything possible to resolve the situation.

- I find it very hard to relax or sleep. People sometimes tell me that I am "high-strung."

- We tend to be impulsive. We take action before considering alternative behaviors or possible consequences. For example:

  - I settle for less than what I really want, because I find it hard to decide.

  - I sometimes write letters that I later wish I could get back.

  - I go places and do things without much planning. I have made many "mistakes" in life.

  - I make commitments that I later regret. I may even have my spouse or children call and cancel my commitments.

  - I find it hard to wait in any line. I prefer to get on a boring ride at the amusement park than wait for the good ride.

STEP ONE

We admitted we were powerless over the effects of our separation from God—that our lives had become unmanageable.

• • •

I know that nothing good lives in me, that is, in my sinful nature. For I have the desire to do what is good, but I cannot carry it out.
(ROM. 7:18)

Understanding Step One

When we were young, we were sometimes tickled by those who were bigger than us. They would often tickle us so hard and long that we lost control. We would gasp and cry for them to stop, and we would scream, "I quit, I give up, please stop!" Sometimes they stopped when we cried and sometimes they stopped only when someone older or bigger came to our rescue.

Step One is like this episode from childhood. Our own life and behavior is like the cruel tickler who inflicts pain and discomfort. We have done this to ourselves. We took control to protect ourselves, but results have frequently ended in chaos. And now we don't want to give up control and release ourselves from the torment. In Step One we admit that we can't stand it anymore. We plead for release. We cry, "I quit!"

Working Step One

We shouldn't look for anything complicated or deep in Step One. Instead, we surrender and face our pain head on. We may have spent a lifetime avoiding, hiding, or medicating the pain. Step One is an opportunity to face reality and admit that our life isn't working with us in control. We embrace our powerlessness and we stop pretending.

Preparing for Step One

The way we manage our own lives brings us to the end of our rope. We hit bottom. Our ways and our efforts fail us. At this point, Step One provides needed direction for our unmanageability. We prepare ourselves by realizing that Step One is the first step in a spiritual journey toward wholeness. This step stops us. It puts a halt to our own efforts and gives us permission to quit.

Prayer for Step One

Today, I ask for help with my recovery. I feel a little lost and am very unsure of myself. Denial has kept me from seeing how powerless I am and how unmanageable my life has become. I need to learn and remember that I cannot manage my life or the lives of others. I also need to remember that the best thing I can do right now is to let go. I choose to let go—I admit that I am powerless and that my life is unmanageable.

The ideas presented in Step One are overwhelming to most of us until we begin to see our lives as they really are. It is threatening to imagine that we could be powerless, and that our lives could be unmanageable. Our life experiences, however, remind us that our behavior does not always produce peace and serenity. Our background, if affected by alcohol or other types of family dysfunction, undermines our best plans, desires, and dreams. Often, our troubled background has caused us to lose touch with God and ourselves. Our lives are full of unwelcome behaviors and overwhelming emotions.

We may have been taught to believe that we only have to accept Christ as our Lord and Savior for our lives to be complete and satisfying. We may have relied upon this to prepare us for the hereafter. Our proclamation that "I am born anew; the past is washed clean; I am a new creature; Christ has totally changed me" is true. Our Spirits are born anew, but since we have a lifetime of habits and wounds, we need more than salvation. We need transformation—the hard work of change. To over- spiritualize the initial work of salvation may be to deny the actual condition of our lives.

The fact that we still feel pain from our past is not a sign of a failed relationship with God. The presence of pain does not lessen the impact of salvation in our lives. This is simply a signal we need to begin the process of healing by daily working the steps with God's help. In time, God will bring the healing and make the necessary changes in our lives. To admit to pains and problems may seem a contradiction of our strong claim to salvation, but it is not. The Bible is full of accounts of men and women who struggled continually to overcome past mistakes and life's many temptations.

The idea that there are areas of our lives over which we are powerless is a new idea for us. It is much easier for us to feel that we have power and are in control. Paul the Apostle, in his letter to the Church of Rome, describes the powerlessness and unmanageability of his life. He writes of his continued sinful behavior as proof of his separation from God (Romans 7:14). Yet, his admission does not interfere with his commitment to do God's will. Without knowing the details of Paul's background, we can only assume from his comments that self-will was a problem. Paul's will got in the way of God's will. Because of our background, we function in much the same way as Paul did, allowing our self-will to work against us.

We live in a culture that places a high value on individual accomplishment. Most of us, from the time we were small children, were bombarded by the ideal of high achievement. Being competitive in school, sports, and business is viewed as important in our society. We are taught that if we compete hard enough we will be "winners" and, therefore, good people. If, however, we don't measure up to what is expected of us and are losers, we believe we are failures. Due to the absence of good role models during childhood, many of us are confused. We don't know where we fit in. We continue to allow our worth and self-esteem to be determined by what we do and what others think of us, and not by who we are in Christ. Looking back at our past, we may continue to classify ourselves as losers. We may condition ourselves to fail. Our low self-esteem keeps us from becoming winners and causes extreme stress and anxiety.

As we mature, matters get worse. The stressful lives we lead give us no satisfaction, and the stress compounds our problems. Our fears and insecurities increase, creating a sense of panic. Some of us revert to abusing mood-altering substances such as drugs, alcohol, or food to relieve our tension. In more subtle ways, we may bury ourselves in church activities, work, relationships, or other addictive/compulsive behaviors to try to combat the anxieties that seem to overwhelm us. When we come to grips with ourselves and realize that our lives are just one big roller-coaster ride, we are ready for Step One. We have no alternative but to admit that we are powerless and that our lives have become unmanageable. When we begin to recognize the seriousness of our condition, it is important that we seek help to stop the roller-coaster.

Step One forms the foundation for working the other steps. In this vital encounter with the circumstances of our lives, we admit our powerlessness and accept the unmanageability of our lives. Surrendering to this idea is not an easy thing to do. Although our behavior has caused us nothing but stress and pain, it is difficult to let go and trust that things will work out well. We may experience confusion, drowsiness, sadness, sleeplessness, or turmoil. These are normal responses to the severe inner struggles we are experiencing. It is important to remember that surrender requires great mental and emotional energy as well as determination. Do not give up. A new life of freedom awaits us.

LOOKING TO SCRIPTURE

In Step One, we come to grips with the reality of our lives. Perhaps for the first time, we finally admit defeat and recognize that we need help. In looking at Step One, we see it has two distinct parts. The first part is the admission that we have obsessive traits. Those traits appear in the way we try to manipulate the affairs of our lives to ease the inner pain of separateness from God. We are in the grip of an addictive process that has rendered us powerless over our behavior. The second part is the admission that our lives have been, and will continue to be, unmanageable if we insist on living by our own will.

I am worn out from groaning; all night long I flood my bed with weeping and drench my couch with tears. My eyes grow weak with sorrow; they fail because of all my foes. PS. 6:6–7

• • •

When we fall away from the plan God has for us, our despair, chaos, and disorder can cause us to feel physically sick and may result in serious illness.

Our self-serving pride cries out against the idea of personal powerlessness and giving up control. We have been accustomed to accepting full responsibility for all that happens in our lives and also in the lives of others. Some of us take on the role of being overly responsible while others of us withdraw and become very irresponsible. Until we reach an intolerable threshold of pain, we will be unable to take the first step toward liberation and renewed strength. The fact that we are powerless is a truth we must realize before we can totally surrender.

This day I call heaven and earth as witnesses against you that I have set before you life and death, blessings and curses. Now choose life, so that you and your children may live and that you may love the Lord your God, listen to his voice, and hold fast to him. DEUT. 30:19–20

• • •

We choose life when we become willing to look at ourselves and our lives honestly, and to seek the help we need for our healing to begin.

Helpful Hint: Read Meditation for Deut. 30:19–20, page 5, *Meditations for The Twelve Steps—A Spiritual Journey.*

As we begin to accept the reality of our condition, we naturally reach out to others for answers. We feel like timid spiritual beginners and wonder why the quality of life we are seeking has escaped us. Friends may tell us, "Read your Bible" or "Pray about it." Some may suggest we talk with our minister. No matter how many outside sources we seek, there will be no relief for us until we, by ourselves, acknowledge our powerlessness. Only then will we begin to see that Step One is the beginning of a way out.

> *The man who thinks he knows something does not yet know as he ought to know.*   1 COR. 8:2
>
> • • •
>
> *Convincing ourselves that our lives are working successfully is a form of denial that prevents us from seeing our condition as it really is.*

Step One is an ongoing commitment. We must remember that our damaging traits, habits, and behaviors are a part of us. They are unconscious reactions to the stresses of life. As we notice self-defeating behaviors and reactions surface, we can admit our powerlessness and seek God's help.

> *That day...they took him along...in the boat. A furious squall came up, and the waves broke over the boat... Jesus was...sleeping on a cushion. The disciples...said to him, "...don't you care if we drown?" He...said to the waves, "Quiet! Be still!" Then the wind died down and it was...calm. He said to his disciples, "Why are you so afraid? Do you still have no faith?"*   MARK 4:35–40
>
> • • •
>
> *Lack of trust and fear of the unknown contribute to our feeling of powerlessness.*

The second part of Step One, admitting that our lives are unmanageable, is as difficult as acknowledging that we are powerless. We can become more observant of the thoughts and behaviors we still rely upon from our past as a way to hide the truth about ourselves today. We need to be totally honest, drop the disguises, and see things as they really are. When we stop finding excuses for our behavior, we will have taken the first step toward achieving the humility we need to accept spiritual guidance. It is through this spiritual guidance that we can begin to rebuild ourselves and our lives.

> Helpful Hint: Read "The Beatitudes", page 61, *Prayers for The Twelve Steps—A Spiritual Journey.*

> **"I am the true vine and my Father is the gardener. He cuts off every branch in me that bears no fruit, while every branch that does bear fruit he trims clean so that it will be even more fruitful.**
>
> JOHN 15:1-2
>
> • • •
>
> *Realizing that we have nonproductive behaviors that damage our health helps us understand why and how our lives have become unmanageable.*

A physical disease can only begin to be healed when we acknowledge its presence. In a similar way, the spiritual healing of our obsessive/compulsive behavior begins when we acknowledge the problem behavior. In Mark 10:51, it was obvious to others that Bartimaeus was blind. However, he openly asked Christ to heal his blindness. Until we realize this truth, our progress toward recovery will be blocked. Our healing begins when we are willing to acknowledge our problems.

> **When he came to his senses, he said, "How many of my father's hired men have food to spare, and here I am starving to death!"** LUKE 15:17
>
> • • •
>
> *When we truly see the reality of our lives and acknowledge our need for help, we invite our Lord into our lives; then the healing process begins.*

As we progress through the Steps, we will discover that true and lasting change does not happen by trying to alter our life conditions. Although it is tempting to think so, outside adjustments cannot correct inside problems. Extraordinary healing requires surrendering the belief that we can heal our lives by manipulating our environment. Our willingness to work the Steps will enable us to begin our true healing, which starts on the inside.

> **"I know that nothing good lives in me, that is, in my sinful nature. For I have the desire to do what is good, but I cannot carry it out. For what I do is not the good I want to do; no, the evil I do not want to do—this I keep on doing. Now if I do what I do not want to do, it is no longer I who do it, but it is sin living in me that does it."**
>
> ROM. 7:18–20
>
> • • •
>
> *No matter how sincere our intentions, we are often powerless to change our behaviors.*

By growing in faith, we become aware that we are not alone. Our Lord said he will not leave us comfortless for he has sent his Holy Spirit. In time, we will come to know his constant presence. For now, each day is a new opportunity to admit our powerlessness and the unmanageability of people, events, and things in our lives.

> *But he said to me, "My grace is sufficient for you, for my power is made perfect in weakness." Therefore I will boast all the more gladly about my weaknesses, so that Christ's power may rest on me. That is why, for Christ's sake, I delight in weaknesses, in insults, in hardships, in persecutions, in difficulties. For when I am weak, then I am strong.*
>
> 2 COR. 12:9–10
>
> • • •
>
> *When we give up our struggle for control and put our lives into God's hands, we find his strength sufficient for every need.*

Helpful Hint: Read Recovery Note for 2 Cor. 11:30 & 12:1–10, *Life Recovery Bible.*

As we begin our journey toward recovery by working the Twelve Steps, old truths will have new meaning for us. We will know what it means when we say we can never be separated from the love of God. Our faith in God and our emerging faith in ourselves and others will sustain us in the steps ahead. This faith serves to strengthen us as we experience the inevitable pain and suffering that our rigorous self-examination will cause. It is the only way out for us—the only way to a new life in Christ. For now, we need only focus on our powerlessness.

> *He who trusts in himself is a fool, but he who walks in wisdom is kept safe.* PROV. 28:26
>
> • • •
>
> *We cannot rely on our will alone; we also must rely on the strength of God working through us.*

KEY IDEAS

Powerless: In Step One we discover that recovery begins with an admission that we are powerless. We admit that we do not have the power to live life as God intends.

Unmanageable: We have tried to manage our lives and the lives of others. However, our management has always met with failure. In Step One we admit that we cannot control or manage our lives any longer.

Dysfunction: If something is functioning normally we understand that it is running the way it is supposed to run. However, *dys*function implies that the function is "impaired" or "abnormal." The Greek prefix *dys* implies "unlucky" or "dangerous." Those of us in recovery understand all too well that our lives have fit these descriptions. We have not been living life as God intended. The functioning of our lives has been ill, bad, unlucky, and even dangerous. Our lives have been *dys*functional.

STEP TWO

Came to believe that a power greater than ourselves could restore us to sanity.

. . .

For it is God who works in you to will and to act according to his good purpose.
(PHIL. 2:13)

Understanding Step Two

"I looked at the white, turbulent waters of the river and melted inside. Any courage I had mustered seeped through my sweating pores. My legs turned to spaghetti at the thought of taking the inflated raft down the rapids—all in the name of fun. Then the river guide, who would steer and command our raft, began to speak. He sounded so sure of himself, so confident that everything would be fine. He gave us instructions, taught us the commands, made us laugh, and even put me at ease. It was crazy, I guess, but I trusted him to make this insane river ride a safe and enjoyable experience."

Step Two is about faith—trust and believing. Faith isn't intellectualized—it just is. Faith isn't manufactured—it's from God. Faith isn't earned—it's a gift. Faith isn't optional—it's a must. Many turbulent and troubled waters await us in our recovery. God knows that, and he prepares us by placing faith in our hearts. When we finally look to God, we will have the faith to believe he is there.

Working Step Two

Step One, if worked properly, leaves us feeling empty. We are left saying, "If I am powerless and cannot manage my life, who can?" God can! God begins to show us his ability by putting a simple seed of faith in our hearts. That seed is simply a growing confidence that someone else, far greater than ourselves, will take charge. Step Two helps us acknowledge the seed of faith that God has given us.

Preparing for Step Two

We prepare for Step Two by acknowledging that we don't know everything about our Higher Power. Many of us have a distorted view of God. We may believe that God is like our abusive or absent parents or significant others. We may believe that God doesn't care how we feel, that he is cruel and waiting to judge us. We may have been threatened with God's punishment all our lives. *"The distorted images that parents place in our hearts and minds carry directly over to our image of God. We grow up feeling that God sees us as our parents did. And so, we grow up seeing ourselves and our God through distorted eyes."*[1] Preparing for Step Two requires that we set aside our old images and mistaken beliefs about God.

Prayer for Step Two

I pray for an open mind so I may come to believe in a power greater than myself. I pray for humility and the continued opportunity to increase my faith. I don't want to be crazy any more.

(Taken from *Prayers for The Twelve Steps—A Spiritual Journey,* page 10)

---

[1] *Divine or Distorted? God as We Understand God,*   Jerry Seiden (San Diego: RPI Publishing, Inc., 1993), pp. 8.

With the help of Step One we came to grips with the fact that we are powerless and our lives are unmanageable. Our next step is to acknowledge the existence of a power greater than ourselves. Believing in God does not always mean that we accept his power. As Christians, we know God, but do not necessarily invite his power into our lives. In Step Two, we have an opportunity to experience God in a different light. Jesus said in John 14:26 that the Holy Spirit would be sent in his name to teach us and remind us of all he has said. In Step Two, we begin to reestablish our relationship, or, establish a relationship with God for the first time. This step gives us an opportunity to experience faith in a power greater than ourselves. This connection will grow and become a vital part of our daily lives.

For many of us, this step presents major obstacles. Since we find it hard to trust others, the loneliness of our present condition causes us to fall back on our own resources. We may even doubt that God can heal us or even be interested in doing so. Unless we let go of our distrust and begin to lean on God, we will continue to operate in an insane manner. The chaos and confusion of our lives will only increase.

Depending on our religious background, some of us may have been taught that God is an authority to be feared. We never saw him as a loving God. As children, we were anxious and feared doing something wrong. Sometimes the threat of being punished by God was used by adults to control our childish behavior. Our fear of displeasing God magnified our growing sense of guilt and shame. As adults, we continue to fear people in authority and are often overcome by guilt and shame for simple misdeeds.

We still may be harboring childhood anger at God because he often disappointed us. Due to the severity of our experiences, some of us rejected God because he did not relieve our pain. Despite our belief that God is with us, in moments of fear we doubt his presence. Even those who are dealing with their problems and are in contact with their Higher Power experience moments of doubt. In Step Two, our goal is to believe that God, a power greater than ourselves, can guide us in our journey toward peace and healing.

For some of us, belief in self-will and our ability to manage our own lives is all we have. We perceive God as a crutch for children and weak-willed individuals who are incapable of managing their own lives. As we begin to see God's true nature, a weight is lifted from our shoulders. We begin to view life from a different perspective.

One of the great paradoxes of Christianity is that man is never completely free until he totally yields to God. In John 8:32, Jesus made a promise when he said, "You shall know the truth and the truth shall make you free." In this step, we begin to recognize that God does, in fact, have the power and intention to alter the course of our lives. In the scriptures, we are assured of God's presence within us. We are shown that through him all things are possible. If we have accepted the truth regarding our condition and have come to believe in our Higher Power, we are well on our way to true spiritual freedom.

Step Two is called "The Hope Step." It gives us new hope as we begin to see that help is available to us. We must simply reach out and accept what our Higher Power has to offer. It is here that we form the foundation for growth of our spiritual life, which will help us become the person we want to be. All we need to do is be willing to believe that a power greater than ourselves is waiting to be our personal salvation. What follows is a process that will bring this power into our lives and enable us to grow in love, health, and grace.

LOOKING TO SCRIPTURE

Coming to believe in a power greater than ourselves requires faith. In the past, we have placed our faith in our own abilities to run our lives, and that faith has proven worthless. It was misplaced and never did for us what we thought it would. Now we need to actively place our faith in God. At first, it may seem unrealistic to place our faith in a power we cannot see or touch. Yet the very existence of our universe in all its glory gives ample evidence of the true power, love, and majesty of the God we seek.

> Helpful Hint: Read Step Two Devotional on "Hope in Faith" from Heb. 11:1–10, *Life Recovery Bible.*

Immediately Jesus made the disciples get into the boat and go on ahead of him to the other side...but the boat was...buffeted by the waves... During the fourth watch of the night Jesus went out to them, walking on the lake. ..."Lord, if it's you," Peter replied, "tell me to come to you on the water." "Come," he said. Then Peter got down out of the boat and walked on the water to Jesus. But when he saw the wind, he was afraid and, beginning to sink, cried out, "Lord, save me!" Immediately Jesus reached out his hand and caught him. "You of little faith," he said, "why did you doubt?" And when they climbed into the boat, the wind died down. Then those who were in the boat worshiped him, saying, "Truly you are the Son of God."

MATT. 14:22–34

• • •

Relying on a power greater than ourselves will give us confidence and hope.

Faith grows through practice. Each time we sense faith and act upon it, our faith becomes stronger. Every time we ask our Higher Power for help and receive it, our faith is strengthened. We will finally accept the fact that God is dependable and will never leave us. All we need to do is ask for help and trust in his power.

> He replied, "Because you have so little faith. I tell you the truth, if you have faith as small as a mustard seed, you can say to this mountain, 'Move from here to there' and it will move. Nothing will be impossible for you."   MATT. 17:20
>
> . . .
>
> With our smallest first step to God, we will experience the comfort he has promised us.

Faith is like a mustard seed. It begins small and grows to influence our lives. To think that little faith is sufficient is wrong. Small mustard seed faith, is just the beginning. Growing, developing, and maturing faith is what we want.

> "If you can?" said Jesus. "Everything is possible for him who believes." Immediately the boy's father exclaimed, "I do believe; help me overcome my unbelief!"   MARK 9:23-24
>
> . . .
>
> Regardless of our past stuggles, we must realize that God's power, not our own, ensures our success.

One great secret of learning to have faith is found in the joyful revelation that the Spirit of God is always within us. God wants to share an intimate relationship with us. God declares that he will never leave us or forsake us. He will be as close to us as we allow him to be.

> *The Lord is close to the brokenhearted and saves those who are crushed in spirit. A righteous man may have many troubles, but the Lord delivers him from them all; he protects all his bones, not one of them will be broken. Evil will slay the wicked; the foe of the righteous will be condemned. The Lord redeems his servants; no one who takes refuge in him will be condemned.* PS. 34:18–22
>
> • • •
>
> *Even though we have rejected him in the past, God will always be close to us and mend our broken spirit.*

We begin to trust our Higher Power as we develop a closer relationship with Jesus Christ. We also begin to rely on him to help us become aware of the extent of our disabling condition. Step Two implies that we are insane. A common definition of insanity in the program is doing the same thing over and over and expecting different results each time. In this sense, we can see our behavior as insane. We still may be blaming everyone and everything for our condition instead of taking responsibility for our own behavior. Or we may still be struggling to control others in order to improve our own lives.

> *Indeed, in our hearts we felt the sentence of death. But this happened that we might not rely on ourselves but on God, who raises the dead.* 2 COR. 1:9
>
> • • •
>
> *However desperate we may be, God's power will relieve our depression and lead us to a new life.*

Our traumatic childhood experiences caused us to become defiant, indifferent, resentful, self-deluded, and self-centered. Our adult lives need to be restored to a more balanced state. We can find that balance if we are willing to believe that God's Holy Spirit is a power greater than ourselves and that he can restore us to sanity. When we attempt to do it alone, we often deceive ourselves by looking to outside sources for the causes of our problems. With the help of Christ, these deceitful behaviors can be healed from the inside out.

> **For it is God who works in you to will and to act according to his good purpose.** PHIL. 2:13
>
> • • •
>
> *God can restore us to wholeness and free us from the hurt and pain of our past.*

One way God helps us see our condition clearly is to bring us into contact with others who share experiences similar to ours. It becomes evident, when sharing our stories in meetings and through fellowship, that each of us can maintain "emotional sobriety" only one day at a time. Also, God helps us realize that actions destructive to ourselves or to others are not acceptable. As we become more dependent on God's power, the quality of our lives will improve and serenity will begin to replace our anxiety.

> **Not that we are competent in ourselves to claim anything for ourselves, but our competence comes from God.** 2 COR. 3:5
>
> • • •
>
> *If we trust him, our Lord will lead us out of the despair we feel when we recognize the dysfunction in our lives.*

Helpful Hint: Read "Possibilities Prayer", page 63, *Prayers for The Twelve Steps—A Spiritual Journey.*

When we started this program, we may have been expecting instant results. From our childhood, we remember feeling anger or confusion when things didn't happen "right now." In this program, sudden change is the exception, not the rule. It requires patience and perseverance to achieve the recovery we seek. Each of us is unique, and recovery begins for each of us at different stages in the steps. Some of us may experience instant relief, whereas others may not begin to feel stronger until later in the program. There is no rule or guideline. Progress occurs at the most appropriate time.

> *Do you not know? Have you not heard? The Lord is the everlasting God, the Creator of the ends of the earth. He will not grow tired or weary, and his understanding no one can fathom. He gives strength to the weary and increases the power of the weak. Even youths grow tired and weary, and young men stumble and fall; but those who hope in the Lord will renew their strength. They will soar on wings like eagles; they will run and not grow weary, they will walk and not be faint.*
>
> ISA. 40:28–31
>
> • • •
>
> *We must work to set aside our impatience and frustration, believing that God will give us sufficient strength to meet our needs.*

Step Two suggests a restoration to sanity. Humility is required to allow this state of mind to unfold. For most of us, lack of humility contributed to our present situation. Humility is a spiritual virtue that we develop with God's help. Developing humility is a recurrent theme of the program. We become humble as we are slowly able to relinquish our pride, self-will, and defiance. In Philippians 2:5 we are told, "Your attitude should be the same as that of Christ Jesus." And Jesus' attitude was one of obedience to do his Father's will, to submit to his Father's plan and power.

> *For I am convinced that neither death nor life, neither angels nor demons, ...neither height nor depth, nor anything else in all creation, will be able to separate us from the love of God that is in Christ Jesus our Lord.* ROM. 8:38–39
>
> • • •
>
> *Neither our pride nor any evil can put us beyond the reach of God's love for us.*

When we become ready to accept our powerlessness and unmanageability (Step One), and when we trust our Higher Power, Jesus Christ, to restore us to sanity (Step Two), we will be ready to make a decision to turn our lives over to the care of God (Step Three). There is no need to rush the process of working the steps. The important thing is to heed the Bible's admonition that "the hour has come for you to wake up from your slumber" (Rom. 13:11). We move forward in faith so we will be able to proceed with the remaining steps. To move forward we need not understand what lies ahead. We only need to trust that God knows the way and he loves us.

> *So do not fear, for I am with you; do not be dismayed, for I am your God. I will strengthen and help you; I will uphold you with my righteous right hand.* ISA. 41:10
>
> • • •
>
> *Our deepening spiritual strength reminds us of God's constant presence in our lives.*

> *For God so loved the world that he gave his one and only Son, that whoever believes in him shall not perish but have eternal life. For God did not send his Son into the world to condemn the world, but to save the world through him.*
>
> JOHN 3:16–17
>
> • • •
>
> *Seen in the light of God's love, the Twelve Steps are a pathway to our wholeness and salvation.*

Helpful Hint: Read Meditation for John 3:16–17, page 27, *Meditations for The Twelve Steps—A Spiritual Journey.*

KEY IDEAS

Higher Power: Because Step One has helped us understand our powerlessness, we need a power beyond ourselves to help and heal us. God is so great and merciful that he does not require that we name him precisely. God is even willing to be anonymous for a time. Remember how God led the Three Wise Men from the East to Christ? The Wise Men did not know the God of Israel or Jesus. They worshiped the stars. So God used a star to lure them. In a similar way, God leads many to himself through the idea of a "Higher Power" in Twelve-Step programs. In Step Two we need to come to believe that there is a loving Higher Power who is willing to help us.

Belief: Belief in something or someone is more than acknowledging that something or someone exists. For example, the Bible says that the demons in Hell believe that God exists, yet that belief doesn't save them (James 2:19). Belief that saves implies trust and commitment. It is one thing to believe that a chair will hold my weight. It is another thing to sit in it. When I sit in the chair, I truly believe in it. In Step Two we come to believe that a power greater than ourselves can restore us to sanity. We do more than acknowledge God's existence: We begin to exercise trust in him to hold us.

Understanding Step Three

Can you imagine the insanity of trying to perform surgery on ourselves? At the first hint of pain from the scalpel, we would stop. Healing would never happen. It is just as insane to think that we can manage our own recovery. We must put our lives into the hands of our Higher Power. God alone knows what is needed for healing. In Step Three we decide to turn the scalpel over to God. We decide to ask him to take control of our will and our lives.

Working Step Three

We work Step Three by going through a decision-making process. Think of other big decisions that we have made in our lives. For example, when making a decision about buying a house, we consider such things about the house as cost, location, condition, etc. We also take into consideration things about ourselves such as our ability to pay, housing needs, personal preferences, etc. Finally, when all things have been weighed, we make a decision. In a similar way we work Step Three. We consider how well the present management of our lives is going. We consider our needs, God's ability, the future. We take time to contemplate the changes. And finally, we make a decision that God is the only one able to manage our lives, that his will for us is best.

Preparing for Step Three

We prepare for Step Three by thoroughly doing Steps One and Two. If we are not convinced that we are powerless and that our lives are unmanageable, we are not ready for Step Three. This step will be difficult if we have not come to believe that God can restore us to sanity and is able to care for us. We prepare for Step Three by fully accepting our powerlessness and our inability to manage our lives. We also prepare by allowing God to plant seeds of faith in our hearts. When those things are in place, Step Three comes easily.

Prayer for Step Three

Lord,
I surrender to you my entire life,
O God of my understanding.
I have made a mess of it
trying to run it myself.
You take, the whole thing,
and run it for me,
According to your will and plan.

(Taken from *Prayers for The Twelve Steps—A Spiritual Journey*, page 13)

Step Three is the central theme of all the steps. It is the point at which we make a decision to turn our will and our lives over to the care of God. Step Three is an important cornerstone for building an effective and peaceful life. In Steps One and Two we established the basis for turning our lives over to the care of God. The commitment we now make in Step Three must be repeated more than once. Actually, we are just beginning to turn things over to God. Repeated working of the first three Steps helps to build a solid foundation for working the total program.

Many of us come to this program with strong negative perceptions about the world in which we live. Those perceptions may be based on hurtful childhood experiences, misguided academic training, or simply the accumulated lessons of our lives. Because of other past experiences, we may have perceived God to be unloving and judgmental. If we have experienced extreme violence as children, we may find it hard to trust anyone or anything—even God. Whatever the source, our recovery is hindered if our beliefs make it difficult to let go of our fear and surrender our lives to God. In Step Three, we decide to take the leap of faith and put our lives in his hands.

Biblical figures often resisted following God's will. The Bible illustrates some examples of doing God's will when it didn't make any sense. Yet, the end result showed it was wise to follow God's guidance. Such acts of faith are exemplified by Moses as he led the nation of Israel into the wilderness and by Abraham's willingness to sacrifice his son Isaac. Also, despite criticism of his contemporaries, Noah built the ark. The essence of these actions is summarized in Hebrews 11:6: *"And without faith it is impossible to please God, because anyone who comes to him must believe that he exists and that he rewards those who earnestly seek him."*

Until now, our inaccurate perceptions of reality have led us into many compulsive/obsessive behaviors. Admitting our responsibility for these dysfunctions is often too difficult. It implies that we have not been "good people." Denial is our only recourse. Our denial acts as a shield against confronting ourselves as we really are. When denial is at work, it is like a shuttered window, closing out the sunlight. In Step Three, we begin the process of opening the shutters and allowing God's light to enter. God's word is a source of light with which we can examine our behavior and understand reality.

Step Three is an affirmative step. It is time to make a decision. In the first two steps, we became aware of our condition and accepted the idea of a power greater than ourselves. Although we began to know and trust God, we may find it difficult to give God total control of our lives. However, if the alternative is to face the loss of people or things vital to our lives, such as family, job, health, or sanity, God's guidance might be easier to accept. Our lives may have many beautiful and rewarding relationships that are being ruined by our addictive/compulsive behavior. We must not be discouraged by these discoveries. Instead, we can allow these discoveries to prompt our surrender to God.

As we begin to allow God's will to act in our lives, our self-destructive tendencies become fewer and much less distracting. Often, the confusion and grief we cause ourselves and others prevent us from successfully working and practicing the steps. Making the decision to begin this journey to health is an act of great importance and should not be made in a time of emotional upheaval. The key elements in Step Three are making the decision with a clear and rational mind, being committed to that decision, and, finally, trusting the outcome to God.

As we surrender our lives and stop carrying the burdens of our past, we will begin to feel better about ourselves.

The more we learn to trust in the Lord, the more we will trust ourselves and extend that trust to others. Our decision to choose God's way will restore us to the fullness of life. As we free ourselves from our self-will, we in turn free ourselves from much of our negative behaviors, and we are able to deal more effectively with the daily routine of our lives. Our impatience and irritability dissipate as we come to know God's love and yearn to share it with others. Our lives transform into a dynamic relationship with God. We become the persons he meant for us to be—full citizens in his kingdom.

LOOKING TO SCRIPTURE

In Step Three, we make an important decision. It is time to acknowledge our need for God's guidance in our lives. We make the decision to surrender our lives to God's care. God becomes our new manager, and we accept life on his terms. He offers us a way to live that is free from the emotional pollution of our past, allowing us to enjoy new and wonderful experiences. Step Three provides us with an opportunity to turn away from behavior that fosters addiction, discouragement, sickness, and fear.

> *Trust in the Lord with all your heart and lean not on your own understanding; in all your ways acknowledge him, and he will make your paths straight.* PROV. 3:5-6
>
> • • •
>
> *When we trust in the Lord and not in ourselves, his guidance will straighten our path.*

Helpful Hint: Read Meditation for Proverbs 3:5-6, page 32, *Meditations for The Twelve Steps—A Spiritual Journey.*

> *Teach me to do your will, for you are my God;*
> *may your good Spirit lead me on level ground.*
>
> PS. 143: 10–11
>
> . . .
>
> *The guidance of the Holy Spirit will bring us peace.*

Many of us begin the Step Three process by deciding to turn over only certain parts of our lives. We are willing to surrender the most difficult problems when we see they are making our lives unmanageable. We cling to other areas of our lives because we think we can manage them. We eventually realize that we cannot barter with God. We must be prepared to surrender our entire will and every part of our lives to his care if we want to recover. When we are truly able to accept this fact, our journey to wholeness has begun.

> *Therefore, I urge you, brothers, in view of God's*
> *mercy, to offer your bodies as living sacrifices,*
> *holy and pleasing to God—which is your spiritual*
> *worship.* ROM. 12:1
>
> . . .
>
> *Surrendering our will and turning our lives over to*
> *God's care will relieve our stress and anxiety.*

Step Three may make us feel we are losing our identity. We may think we are going to lose everything. Not knowing what is going to happen is frightening. Most of us have tried desperately to control our environment. Many of these behavior traits were developed during childhood and came about as a direct result of the circumstances in which we were raised. Deep within us may be a fearful childhood memory and a trembling child, anxious about someone's anger, criticism, threats, or violence. As children, we tried to fix or take care of the people around us so they would not abandon us, leaving us with only broken promises and shattered dreams. As a result, we reinforced in ourselves a host of undesirable tendencies such as caretaking, controlling, and an overdeveloped sense of responsibility.

> *Yet to all who received him, to those who believed in his name, he gave the right to become children of God—children born not of natural descent, nor of human decision or a husband's will, but born of God.* JOHN 1:12-13
>
> • • •
>
> Our childhood relationship with God is still an influence we must deal with in learning to trust that our true Father is God.

The conditions in which we were raised often kept us from ever trusting in God. Our prayers may have been unanswered, and we could not imagine how a loving God could be so cruel to us. Step Three is an opportunity to start over.

As we work the Steps, we will get in touch with memories of childhood hurts. We also will begin to experience God's healing love, which transcends time, to repair the damage that has been done. Jesus told us that we must become like children to enter the Kingdom of God. This statement helps us recognize that a childlike state will enable us to regain our capacity to give and receive unconditional love. Thus, we can look forward to a return of childlike spontaneity, and a growing capacity to give and receive love and nurturing

> *"Come to me, all you who are weary and burdened, and I will give you rest. Take my yoke upon you and learn from me, for I am gentle and humble in heart, and you will find rest for your souls. For my yoke is easy and my burden is light."*
>
> MATT. 11:28–30
>
> • • •
>
> *The Lord wants us to give him the burdens of guilt and shame we have carried with us since childhood.*

Helpful Hint: Read "Prayers of Submission," Chapter Six, pages 85–92, *Prayers for The Twelve Steps—A Spiritual Journey.*

Learning to trust in God and accept his support will enhance the quality of our lives. We will no longer feel the need to carry our burdens by ourselves. Much of the pain of our past is a result of feeling totally alone. With God's presence, our sense of self-esteem will improve, and we will begin to recognize that we are worthwhile human beings. Our capacity to receive and give love will increase, and we will come to place great value on fellowship and sharing.

> *It is better to take refuge in the Lord than to trust in man. It is better to take refuge in the Lord than to trust in princes.*   PS. 118:8–9
>
> • • •
>
> *Our growing trust in God will give us courage to extend love to ourselves and others.*

Christ exemplified the concept of "turning it over" by acceptance of his Father's will, which led to the Cross and the victory of resurrection. During his life on earth, Jesus' love for us led him into constant confrontations with the forces of evil. He was strong and steadfast in those confrontations because he placed his trust in his Heavenly Father. But Jesus had confrontations of a different nature: confrontations within himself. He struggled with doing God's will because it wasn't always the easy way. Even Jesus expressed his struggle in prayer, yet he always yielded to his Father's will because he knew it was best.

> *Going a little farther, he fell with his face to the ground and prayed, "My Father, if it is possible, may this cup be taken from me. Yet not as I will, but as you will."* MATT. 26:39
>
> • • •
>
> *Whatever trials we face, we are not alone. We are united with God through Christ, whose love always triumphs over evil.*

In this life, we too have crosses to bear. Some of us still may be experiencing the powerful impact of our history of disabling behavior. Whether our addiction is drugs, destructive relationships, sex, alcohol, money, or food, we face the possibility of spiritual as well as physical death. As we turn away from these temptations, we accept God's offer to cast our burdens upon him.

> *I have been crucified with Christ and I no longer live, but Christ lives in me. The life I live in the body, I live by faith in the Son of God, who loved me and gave himself for me.* GAL.2:20
>
> • • •
>
> *When Christ lives in us, we can acknowledge and defeat temptation.*

When we develop a daily routine of working Step Three, a change will come over us. We will be calmer and feel less responsible for everything and everybody. Peace and serenity will come to us in measures never before experienced. Our eyes will be opened, and we will have a fresh start in life. We will become increasingly aware that God is guiding us. People around us may notice that we have become more confident and trustworthy.

> **Commit to the Lord whatever you do, and your plans will succeed.**   PROV. 16:3
>
> • • •
>
> *God leads us to victory over the trials of this life, so that we may experience success through his strength.*

No matter how far we progress in recovery, we must continually turn our lives over to the care of God and be vigilant. It is foolish for us not to anticipate relapses. We need only to recognize this, and to willingly work the program on a daily basis. It is especially important to continue to practice Step Three. Our willingness to trust in God ensures our victory. Without it, we resort to our old survival techniques and traits, and we place ourselves back in control.

> **I tell you the truth, anyone who has faith in me will do what I have been doing. He will do even greater things than these, because I am going to the Father. And I will do whatever you ask in my name, so that the Son may bring glory to the Father.**   JOHN 14:12–13
>
> • • •
>
> *The improvements we begin to see in our lives are the first fruits of the goodness God has in store for us.*

"For I know the plans I have for you," declares the Lord, "plans to prosper you and not to harm you, plans to give you hope and a future. Then you will call upon me and come and pray to me, and I will listen to you. You will seek me and find me when you seek me with all your heart. I will be found by you," declares the Lord.

JER. 29:11–14

. . .

When working Step Three, we discover the depth of God's love for us and understand that through him all things are possible.

Helpful Hint: Read Recovery Note for Jer. 29:11, *Life Recovery Bible.*

Thousands of people seeking to experience peace, serenity, and fellowship with the Lord have walked this same path. Our task is to continually ask God for guidance. We receive his guidance by personal invitation. Jesus said, *"Here I am! I stand at the door and knock. If anyone hears my voice and opens the door, I will come in and eat [fellowship] with him, and he with me."* (Rev. 3:20) All we need to do is open the door of our hearts to Christ. The following prayer can help our relationship with Christ and strengthen our daily walk:

Lord Jesus,
I turn my will and my life over to you.
Mold me and do with me as you will.
I trust you to guide my steps, and
I enter the world with hope that I may better do your will.
I ask for your forgiveness and acceptance.
I welcome your Holy Spirit's power, love, and guidance
in everything I do. Amen.

KEY IDEAS

Turn It Over: This phrase of surrender is a key idea for Step Three. Imagine turning over your car keys to someone else. Think of turning over a job or a responsibility to a more capable person. People who have been in the program for any length of time talk about turning over problems and daily troubles to their Higher Power. For those of us who are working Step Three for the first time, we are turning over our will and our lives to God's care. Whatever imagery you choose, let the meaning always be the same: the surrender of your will and life. Turn it over. Give God control.

Self-will: Self-will is the determination within us all to control our own lives. Self-will in itself is not wrong; God has given us the power to choose. The problem with choice occurs when our will conflicts with God's. Our choices have brought us pain, hardships, addictions, compulsions, and self-defeating behaviors. God's will for our lives brings us hope, healing, and peace. His plans are good. Our self-will is best exercised in choosing surrender to God.

Understanding Step Four

If we lived alone and were unable to see, we would be faced with a number of special needs. For example, we might find it difficult to clean our home thoroughly by ourselves. We might ask a sighted friend to come over and help. This friend would see areas in need of cleaning that we had missed. Our friend would point these problems out and then, we hope, help us clean them.

In Step Four we realize there are areas of our lives that need attention. We also realize that we cannot see all those areas. Denial has kept us blinded to the dirt in our corners. Low self-esteem has kept us ignorant about the beauty and worth of our lives. In this step, our Higher Power comes to us as a caring friend. God opens our eyes to the weaknesses in our lives that need changing and helps us to build on our strengths.

Working Step Four

Just as any business would take inventory of its stock, we take inventory of our lives in Step Four. With clipboard in hand, we walk down the aisles of our lives and note areas of weakness and strength. When we come to relationships, we take stock of the resentments and grudges, but we also examine our loving and healthy relationships. When we come to our communication, we note the lies, but we also list the positive ways we share with others. In this process we can look to God for guidance. He knows the contents of our warehouse far better than we do.

Preparing for Step Four

We prepare for Step Four by recognizing the fact that, to some degree, denial has been operating in our lives. We prepare by asking God for the courage to face those areas that have been protected by denial. And we prepare for Step Four by planning to nurture ourselves during and after the inventory process.

Prayer for Step Four

Dear God,
It is I who have made my life a mess. I have done it, but I cannot undo it. My mistakes are mine, and I will begin a searching and fearless moral inventory. I will write down my wrongs, but I will also include that which is good. I pray for the strength to complete the task.

(Taken from *Prayers for The Twelve Steps—A Spiritual Journey,* page 14)

S tep Four begins the growth steps of our journey. Here, we examine our behavior and expand our understanding of ourselves. The adventure of self-discovery begins with Step Four and continues through Step Seven. During these next four steps, we will prepare a personal inventory, discuss it with others in the program, and invite God to remove our shortcomings. Being totally honest in preparing our inventory is vital to the self-discovery that forms the foundation of our recovery. This honesty allows us to remove the obstacles that have prevented us from knowing ourselves and truthfully acknowledging our deepest feelings about life.

Step Four helps us get in touch with our "shadow," that part of us that we have hidden away for so long—our repressed nature. In the process of making our inventory, we will develop and broaden our understanding of our behavior. We will see that our "shadow" is an integral part of our nature and must be accepted by us. This part of our nature hides our resentments, fears, and other repressed feelings. As we begin to see ourselves, we will learn to accept our whole character—the good and the bad. This acceptance will free us to discover survival behaviors that began in childhood. In the context of our turbulent early years, these behaviors were lifesaving. However, their continuation into our adulthood renders us dysfunctional.

Denial is a key survival skill that we learned early in childhood. It stunted our emotional growth by keeping us in a make-believe world. We often fantasized that our situation was better than it really was. Denial protected us from our feelings and helped us repress the pain of our family environment. Our shame and guilt caused us to be silent, rather than to be honest and face the fear of being ridiculed by others. This withdrawal hindered us from developing into mature, emotionally healthy adults. As our self-discovery unfolds, we begin to recognize the role that denial has played in our lives. This realization is the basis for our acceptance of the truth of our personal history.

Resentment and fear are two issues that need to be dealt with before we can begin the process of preparing our inventory. Our resentment toward people, places, and things that have injured us keeps us preoccupied and limits our ability to live in the present moment. Resentment results from hiding the bitter hurts that have tarnished our lives. It evokes anger, frustration, and depression. When our resentments are unresolved, we risk developing severe physical and mental illnesses.

Fear limits our ability to be rational. When fear is present, it is difficult to see situations in their true perspective. Fear is the root of other repressive and painful feelings. It prevents us from expressing ourselves honestly and stops us from responding in appropriate ways to threatening situations. So to change our behavior, we must first face and accept our fears. By acknowledging our fearful nature, we can expect a temporary loss of self-esteem; fortunately, this will return as we become more willing to rely on God.

Preparing our inventory requires that we look to God for guidance. We renewed our relationship to our Higher Power in Steps Two and Three, and now we ask God for help. We will look closely at our personal histories and acknowledge what we see in them. As the process unfolds, we will recognize the need for change. This task will be much easier if we just remember that God is with us. With God's help, we can courageously review our strengths and our weaknesses.

Step Four gives us the opportunity to recognize that certain skills, acquired in childhood, may be inappropriate in our adult lives. Blaming others for our misfortunes, denying responsibility for hurtful behavior, and resisting the truth are behavior patterns we must discard. These particular learned behaviors were developed early in life and have become character defects. We look at them now and feel troubled. Painful memories may return. Our willingness to be honest about what we uncover will give us the clarity of mind that is vital for our continued recovery.

Putting our thoughts on paper is valuable and necessary when completing Step Four. The process of writing focuses our wandering thoughts and allows us to concentrate on what is really happening. It often causes repressed feelings to surface and gives us a deeper understanding of ourselves and our behavior. We need to accept whatever we discover, knowing that this discovery is merely another step toward a healthier life. We must be honest and thorough to complete Step Four successfully. With God's help and our personal courage, we can expect to receive limitless benefits.

LOOKING TO SCRIPTURE

Denial stems from our childhood environment, which we were unable to control. This was our way of dealing with the confusion, instability, and violence of the adults around us. We rationalized what was happening and invented acceptable reasons for their unacceptable behavior. By doing this, we ignored the chaos and denied the overwhelming problems. As we matured, our denial continued to protect us from the need to face reality.

> *"The heart is deceitful above all things and beyond cure. Who can understand it? "I the Lord search the heart and examine the mind, to reward a man according to his conduct, according to what his deeds deserve."*   JER. 17:9–10
>
> • • •
>
> *Attempting to survive the chaos by denying its existence fosters deceit and illusion.*

The power of denial is illustrated in the Bible when Peter denies Christ. Because of his great love for Christ, Peter thought it inconceivable that he could deny Christ. However, when Peter was confronted with the situation, it was easier for him to deny Christ than it was to admit being a follower and face the consequences. When Peter realized what he had done, he was devastated. In much the same way, when we realize what denial has done to us, we experience feelings of self-hatred, which need to be acknowledged and resolved.

> *While Peter was below in the courtyard, one of the servant...saw Peter warming himself..."You also were with that Nazarene, Jesus," she said. But he denied it...and went out into the entry way. When the servant saw him there, she said again to those standing around, "this fellow is one of them."...He began to call down curses on himself, and swore... Immediately the rooster crowed...And he broke down and wept.*   MARK 14:66–72
>
> • • •
>
> *When we fear the consequences of telling the truth, we are inclined to tell lies.*

Denial has many faces and can be easily masked. Some recognizable forms are:

Simple Denial: To pretend that something does not exist when it really does (e.g., discounting physical symptoms that may suggest the presence of problems).

Minimizing: To acknowledge a problem, but refuse to see its severity (e.g., admitting to an overusage of prescription drugs when in fact there is overt addiction).

Blaming: To recognize the problem, then blame someone else for its cause (e.g., blaming others for your tendency to isolate).

Excusing: To offer excuses, alibis, justifications, and other explanations for our own or others' behavior (e.g., calling in sick for a partner when the actual cause of the absence is drunkenness).

Generalizing: To deal with problems on a general level, which typically avoids personal and emotional awareness of the situation or conditions (e.g., sympathizing with a friend's unemployment when you know the underlying cause is irresponsibility).

Dodging: To change the subject to avoid threatening topics (e.g., talking about the weather when your spouse is discussing the overdrawn checkbook).

Attacking: To become angry when reference is made to the existing condition, thus avoiding the issue (e.g., arguing about work conditions when the boss addresses tardiness).

> *If anyone thinks he is something when he is nothing, he deceives himself. Each one should test his own actions. Then he can take pride in himself, without comparing himself to somebody else, for each one should carry his own load.* GAL. 6:3–5
>
> • • •
>
> *Our pride can limit our capacity to be honest and is a critical element in making our searching and fearless moral inventory.*

Helpful Hint: Read Recovery Note for Gal. 6:1–3, *Life Recovery Bible.*

Taking a personal inventory is similar to cleaning a closet. We take stock of what we have, examine what we want to save, and discard what is no longer useful or appropriate.

It doesn't have to be done all at once, but it must be done eventually. If we take small sections at a time, the cleaning is more thorough and the long-term results are better. In the same way that clothes can trigger memories of the past, our inventory may provoke both positive and negative memories. We must remember that the past is only history. It is not the purpose of our inventory to dwell on the past. Nor is it to examine the past for purposes of assigning or accepting blame. This reflection is only a tool to help us understand our current behavior patterns. Reflection on the past can give us insights into our present struggles and our enduring weaknesses. Our main concern now is for our future. We can lessen our fears surrounding this task by approaching the inventory in this manner.

> **Let us examine our ways and test them, and let us return to the Lord.**   LAM. 3:40
>
> • • •
>
> *Personal examination of our lives will give us insight into the ways in which we have turned away from God and become self-destructive.*

In Step Four, we will get in touch with many behaviors and attitudes that have been with us since childhood. Our growing awareness about the way we were raised will help us understand that our present behaviors are natural out-growths of our early need to survive. As adults, we now can choose a different lifestyle for ourselves. We can learn to conduct ourselves in a way that is nurturing to us. As we look at our strengths and weaknesses, we will become aware of the areas of our lives that need to be strengthened. We can use the inventory to decide which areas of our lives need changing, and which areas seem the way we want them to be.

Search me, O God, and know my heart; test me and know my anxious thoughts. See if there is any offensive way in me, and lead me in the way everlasting. PS. 139:23–24

. . .

We extend our trust in God by asking him to be part of our process of self-discovery.

Our next task is to look at resentment and recognize how damaging it is to us. It is the number one offender and often the major cause of spiritual disease. As we list our resentments, we see how they have affected our self-esteem, our well-being, and our personal relationships. Holding on to resentment causes stress, anxiety, and uncontrollable feelings of anger. If these are unresolved, serious emotional and physical consequences will develop. If we allow our resentments to prevail, serious depression can develop and ultimately destroy us.

My dear brothers, take note of this: Everyone should be quick to listen, slow to speak and slow to become angry, for man's anger does not bring about the righteous life that God desires. Therefore, get rid of all moral filth and the evil that is so prevalent, and humbly accept the word planted in you, which can save you. JAMES 1:19–21

. . .

Resentment and anger keep us focused on the person or situation causing the negative feelings and prevent us from accepting God's promise of healing.

The second most destructive offender is fear. It is the emotion we most strongly feel when we begin to look at ourselves. When fear is present, our need to deny, ignore, and avoid reality increases. Our unrealistic perspective becomes greatly exaggerated and intensifies our emotional responses. Fear can cause us much pain. It attacks us physically and causes feelings that range from apprehension to panic. When fear is present, we may become nervous, nauseated, or disoriented. As we inventory our fears, we may discover that they are a direct result of our inability to make decisions.

> *There is no fear in love. But perfect love drives out fear, because fear has to do with punishment. The one who fears is not made perfect in love.*
> 1 JOHN 4:18
> . . .
> *The guilt and shame we feel about our past behaviors may inhibit our ability to conduct a thorough inventory. God's love for us will remove our fear.*

Facing our resentments and fears requires a great deal of courage. Our past tendency has been to shut down our feelings. Now we begin to look at areas of our lives that we have never explored before. It is important to realize that God is with us and will help us every step of our way. With God's help and understanding, the pain will diminish.

> *Examine yourselves to see whether you are in the faith; test yourselves. Do you not realize that Christ Jesus is in you—unless, of course, you fail the test? And I trust that you will discover that we have not failed the test.*
> 2 COR. 13:5–6
> . . .
> *Our faith grows as we examine ourselves and see how Jesus Christ is present in our lives.*

> Helpful Hint: Read Meditation for 2 Cor. 13:5–6, page 54, *Meditations for The Twelve Steps—A Spiritual Journey.*

As part of the Step Four inventory, we will look at our character traits and see our strengths and weaknesses. Our strengths appear in behavior that has positive effects on us as well as on others, weaknesses are revealed in behavior that is destructive. Understanding begins when we discover how we became the people we are—how we formulated the ideas, beliefs, and attitudes that govern how we act.

> *Get rid of all bitterness, rage and anger, brawling and slander, along with every form of malice.*
>
> EPH. 4:31
>
> • • •
>
> *Unexpressed feelings will contaminate the peace and serenity for which we strive.*

Our inventory may prove difficult. If we are blocked, denial may be operating. We need to stop for a moment, reflect on what we are attempting to do, and analyze our feelings. We must also ask God for help. In times like this, God's presence means a gread deal to us, and we must be willing to look to him for support.

> *I remember my affliction and my wandering, the bitterness and the gall. I well remember them, and my soul is downcast within me. Yet this I call to mind and therefore I have hope: Because of the Lord's great love we are not consumed, for his compassion never fail.*
>
> LAM. 3:19–22
>
> • • •
>
> *God's love will lead us through the darkness of the past and into the light of a new life.*

Blessed is the man who perseveres under trial, because when he has stood the test, he will receive the crown of life that God has promised to those who love him.   JAMES 1:12

• • •

Our courage grows as we complete our personal inventory and triumph over the temptation to avoid facing the truth of our past.

The inventory we are preparing is for our own benefit, not the benefit of others. It will help us make a major breakthrough in our self-acceptance and lead us further along the road to recovery. As we go to Steps Five, Six, and Seven, the process continues to unfold as we acknowledge the truth about ourselves, discuss it with others, and, finally, ask God to remove our shortcomings.

Put to death, therefore, whatever belongs to your earthly nature: sexual immorality, impurity, lust, evil desires and greed, which is idolatry. Because of these, the wrath of God is coming. You used to walk in these ways, in the life you once lived. But now you must rid yourselves of all such things as these: anger, rage, malice, slander, and filthy language from your lips.   COL. 3:5–8

• • •

Our Fourth Step inventory will help us realize how far we have strayed from God's way. It is our first step toward putting the past to rest.

Helpful Hint: Read "I Need to Take a Trip," page 14–15, *Prayers for The Twelve Steps—A Spiritual Journey.*

KEY IDEAS

Moral Inventory: A moral inventory is a list of our weaknesses and our strengths. In this text the weaknesses are also referred to as wrongs, character defects, faults, and shortcomings. This inventory is something we prayerfully accomplish with God's help. It is for our benefit.

Survival Skills: Survival skills are those familiar defenses that we developed to protect ourselves from the chaos of our childhood homes. These early childhood survival skills followed us into adult life and added to our struggles.

Denial: Denial is a key survival skill that we learned in early childhood. We protect ourselves by pretending that nothing is wrong and that our lives are fulfilling. We ignore the real problems by replacing them with elaborate explanations, rationalizations, and distractions such as minimizing, blaming, excusing, generalizing, dodging, and attacking.

Resentment: Resentment is a major roadblock to recovery that must be removed. Resentment is the bitterness and anger we feel toward those whom we perceive as threats to our security or well-being or those who have caused us harm. If not removed, our resentments hinder our progress and growth.

Fear: Fear is often our first response to anything new. We meet change with fear because we feel threatened by so many things. Fear creates a physical response that begins with the release of adrenaline and ends with the whole body on alert. This alerted state often leads to persistent and unwanted tension and can develop into stress-related illness.

Shadow: Although "shadow" may sound odd or like unfamiliar Christian terminology, the idea of a battle between light and dark is a biblical truth. When St. John speaks of Christ's coming, he describes Christ as light. The idea of darkness and shadow illustrates the evil side of this world and the corrupt nature in ourselves. "Shadow" refers to the darkness we carry within us. Just as our shadow follows our every move, our dark side or fallen nature is always with us. Our shadow is most evident when contrasted with the light of day. Our old, fallen nature is very noticeable when we stand beside God's light, the Bible. Take time to read John 1:1–9, Romans 7:7–25, and 1 John 1:5–7.

IMPORTANT GUIDELINES IN PREPARING YOUR INVENTORY

The materials offered in this Step Four Inventory Guide is different from the inventory guides used in other Twelve-Step programs. They emphasize those feelings and behaviors most commonly seen in adults from homes where substance abuse or other damage-inducing behavior was prevalent. When preparing your inventory, choose the traits that specifically apply to you. Don't tackle them all at once. For now, only work on the ones that you feel comfortable doing. Come back to the difficult ones later. Focus on recent events and record words and actions as accurately as possible. Take your time. It's better to be thorough with some than incomplete with all.

The inventory begins with exercises on resentments and fears, followed by a series of feelings and behaviors to be examined. This process prepares you for Step Five. You are the primary beneficiary of your honesty and thoroughness in this inventory. It is important to refrain from generalizing. Be as specific as possible.

Following the section on character weaknesses there is an opportunity to list your character strengths. This chapter also includes an "Additional Inventory" to record your weaknesses and strengths that were not listed in the text.

NOTE: Step Ten includes a special inventory to measure your progress from the Step Four inventory.

RESENTMENT

Resentment is an underlying cause of many forms of spiritual disease. Our mental and physical ills are frequently the direct result of this unhealthy condition. No doubt others have harmed us, and we have a legitimate right to feel resentful. However, resentment doesn't punish anyone but ourselves. We can't hold resentments and find healing at the same time. It's best released by asking God for the strength to forgive the offender. Learning to deal with resentment in a healthy way is an important part of our recovery process.

When we resent, we may be:

Feeling injured	Feeling left out
Feeling violated	Retaliating
Experiencing low self-worth	Angry/Bitter

Consider situations where resentment is a problem for you.

Example: **I resent** my boss **because** he doesn't care to hear my explanation of why I am depressed. **This affects** my self-esteem. **This activates** unexpressed anger. **This makes me feel** even more depressed.

Self-Evaluation: On a scale from one to ten, how much does resentment negatively affect your life? Number one indicates that it has little negative effect. Number ten indicates that it has great negative effect. Circle where you are today.

| 1 | 2 | 3 | 4 | 5 | 6 | 7 | 8 | 9 | 10 |

FEAR

Fear is an underlying cause of many forms of spiritual disease. It is the first response we feel when we aren't in control of a situation. A wide range of mental and physical ills are frequently the direct result of this unwholesome emotion. Fear often prevents us from seeing options to effectively resolve the issues causing the fear. Learning to acknowledge fear in a healthy way is an important part of our recovery process.

When we fear, we may be:

Feeling threatened	Resisting change
Fighting for survival	Facing our mortality
Experiencing rejection	Anticipating loss

Consider situations where fear is a problem for you.

Example: **I fear** my spouse **because** I feel that I am never able to please him/her. **This affects** my self-esteem and sexuality. **This activates** my fear of abandonment. **This makes me feel** worthless and angry.

Self-evaluation: On a scale from one to ten, how much does fear negatively affect your life? Number one indicates that it has little negative effect. Number ten indicates that it has great negative effect. Circle where you are today.

1	2	3	4	5	6	7	8	9	10

INAPPROPRIATE ANGER

Anger is a major source of many problems in the lives of adults who were reared in chaotic homes. It is a feeling that we often suppress, because admitting it makes us uncomfortable. In our chaotic homes, the turmoil was so intense that we either denied our anger or expressed it inappropriately. We felt it was safer to protect ourselves and simply hoped our feelings would go away. We were not aware that repressed anger could lead to serious resentment and depression. It causes physical complications that can develop into stress-related illnesses. Denying anger or expressing it inappropriately causes problems in relationships because we cannot be truthful about our feelings and must always be pretending.

When we inappropriately express anger, we may experience:

Resentment	Depression
Self-Pity	Jealousy
Anxiety	Stress

Consider situations where anger is a problem for you.

Example: **I inappropriately express anger** toward my son **because** I am embarrassed by his behavior. **This affects** my self-worth. **This activates** my fear of rejection. **This makes me feel** imcompetent as a parent.

Self-Evaluation: On a scale from one to ten, how much does anger negatively affect your life? Number one indicates that it has little negative effect. Number ten indicates that it has great negative effecte. Circle where you are today.

| 1 | 2 | 3 | 4 | 5 | 6 | 7 | 8 | 9 | 10 |

APPROVAL   SEEKING

Because of our dysfunctional upbringing, we fear disapproval and criticism. As children, we desperately wanted to receive approval from our parents, grandparents, siblings, and significant others. As a result we were constantly seeking validation of ourselves. This need for approval continued into adulthood and seriously affected the way we pattern our lives and thinking around the needs of others. Rather than look for approval in a positive way, we seek validation in order to feel better about ourselves. This keeps us out of touch with our own feelings and desires, and prevents us from discovering our own wants and needs. We look for reactions in others, and attempt to manage their impression of us. We constantly strive to please everyone and often stay in relationships that are destructive to us.

When we need approval from others, we may be:

People pleasing   Feeling unworthy
Fearing criticism   Ignoring our own needs
Fearing failure   Lacking confidence

Consider situations where approval seeking is a problem for you.

Example: **I seek approval** from my friends **because** I want to feel better about myself. **This affects** my relationship with my friends. **This activates** my fear of rejection. **This makes me feel** like I'm not important to anyone.

Self-evaluation: On a scale from one to ten, how much does approval seeking negatively affect your life? Number one indicates that it has little negative effect. Number ten indicates that it has great negative effect. Circle where you are today.

| 1 | 2 | 3 | 4 | 5 | 6 | 7 | 8 | 9 | 10 |

CARETAKING

As children, we frequently assumed the responsibility for concerns and problems of others that were far beyond our capability to handle. As a result, we were deprived of a normal childhood. The unrealistic demands placed on us, and the praise we received for being "little adults," made us believe we had Godlike powers. Taking care of others boosted our self-esteem and made us feel indispensable. It gave purpose to our lives. As caretakers, we are most comfortable with chaotic situations where others assure us that we are needed. Although we often resent others for taking and not giving, we are unable to allow others to care for us. We don't experience the joy of taking care of ourselves.

As caretakers, we may:

Feel indispensable	Lose our identity
Rescue people	Feel very responsible
Ignore our own needs	Be co-dependent

Consider situations where caretaking is a problem for you.

Example: **I take care of** my boyfriend's financial problems **because** I want him to love me more. **This affects** available funds for my own financial needs. **This activates** my resentment and tendency to withdraw. **This makes me feel** very lonely.

Self-evaluation: On a scale from one to ten, how much does caretaking negatively affect your life? Number one indicates that it has little negative effect. Number ten indicates that it has little negative effect. Circle where you are today.

1	2	3	4	5	6	7	8	9	10

CONTROL

As children, we had little or no control over our environment or the events that took place in our lives. As adults, we have extraordinary needs to control our feelings and behavior, and we try to control the feelings and behavior of others. We become rigid and unable to have spontaneity in our lives. We trust only ourselves to complete a task or to handle a situation. We manipulate others in order to gain their approval and keep a balance of control that makes us feel safe. We fear that our lives will deteriorate if we give up our management position. We become stressed and anxious when our authority is threatened.

Due to our need to be in control, we may:

Overreact to change	Be judgmental and rigid
Lack trust	Be intolerant
Fear failure	Manipulate others

Consider situations where control is a problem for you.

Example: **I control** my nineteen-year-old son **because** I am afraid of losing him. **This affects** my relationship with him. **This activates** my fear of abandonment. **This makes me feel** very frightened and powerless.

Self-evaluation: On a scale from one to ten, how much does control negatively affect your life? Number one indicates that it has little negative effect. Number ten indicates that it has great negative effect. Circle where you are today.

1	2	3	4	5	6	7	8	9	10

FEAR OF ABANDONMENT

Fear of abandonment is a reaction to stress that we developed in early childhood. As children, we observed unpredictable behavior from responsible adults. We never knew from one day to the next if our parents would be there for us. Many of us were abandoned either physically or emotionally. As our parents' addictions increased in severity, their inability to parent also increased. As children, we simply were not important. Now as adults, we are inclined to choose partners with whom we can repeat this pattern. We try to be perfect by meeting all our partner's needs in order to avoid experiencing the pain of abandonment. Our need to reduce the possibility of abandonment takes precedence over dealing with issues or conflicts. This behavior produces a tense environment with poor communication.

When we fear abandonment, we may:

Feel insecure	Worry excessively
Become caretakers	Become co-dependent
Avoid being alone	Feel rejected

Consider situations where fear of abandonment is a problem for you.

Example: **I fear abandonment** by my husband **because** he doesn't pay much attention to me. **This affects** my peace of mind. **This activates** my caretaking and manipulation of him. **This makes me feel** very frightened and vulnerable.

Self-evaluation: On a scale from one to ten, how much does fear of abandonment negatively affect your life? Number one indicates that it has little negative effect. Number ten indicates that it has great negative effect. Circle where you are today.

1	2	3	4	5	6	7	8	9	10

FEAR OF AUTHORITY FIGURES

Fear of people in roles of authority can be a result of our parents' unrealistic expectations of us—wanting us to be more than we were able to be. We see people in authority as having unrealistic expectations of us and thus, we fear we cannot meet their expectations. We are unable to deal with people whom we perceive as being in positions of power. Simple assertiveness displayed by others is often misinterpreted by us as anger. This can cause us to feel intimidated and to become oversensitive. No matter how competent we are, we compare ourselves to others and conclude that we are inadequate. As a result, we constantly compromise our integrity in order to avoid confrontation or criticism.

Fear of authority figures may cause us to:

Fear rejection	Compare ourselves to others
Take things personally	React rather than act
Be arrogant	Feel inadequate

Consider situations where authority figures are a problem for you.

Example: **I fear** my boss **because** I don't want her to know how stupid I think I am. **This affects** my actions when I am around her. **This activates** my need to isolate—I try to be unnoticed. **This makes me feel** childish and immature.

Self-evaluation: On a scale from one to ten, how much does fear of authority figures negatively affect your life? Number one indicates that it has little negative effect. Number ten indicates that it has great negative effect. Circle where you are today.

1	2	3	4	5	6	7	8	9	10

FROZEN FEELINGS

Many of us have difficulty expressing our feelings or even realizing that we have them. We harbor deep emotional pain and a sense of guilt and shame. As children, our feelings were met with disapproval, anger, and rejection. For survival purposes, we learned to hide our feelings or repress them entirely. As adults, we are not in touch with our feelings. We can only allow ourselves to have "acceptable" feelings to stay "safe." Our true nature is distorted so we can protect ourselves from the reality of what is truly happening. Distorted and repressed feelings cause resentment, anger, and depression, which often lead to physical illness.

When we have frozen feelings, we may:

Be unaware of our feelings	Be depression
Have distorted feelings	Withhold conversation
Suppress positive feelings	Struggle with relationships

Consider situations where frozen feelings are a problem for you.

Example: **I repress my feelings** toward my spouse **because** I don't want to be hurt. **This affects** my actions and limits my ability to communicate with my spouse. **This activates** my need to isolate and causes me to be accused of being insensitive and unaffectionate. **This makes me feel** very isolated and lonely.

Self-evaluation: On a scale from one to ten, how much do frozen feelings negatively affect your life? Number one indicates that they have little negative effect. Number ten indicates that they have great negative effect. Circle where you are today.

1	2	3	4	5	6	7	8	9	10

ISOLATION

We usually find it safer to withdraw from surroundings that are uncomfortable for us. By isolating ourselves, we prevent others from seeing us as we really are. We tell ourselves that we are not worthy and, therefore, do not deserve love, attention, or acceptance. We also tell ourselves that we cannot be punished or hurt if we don't express our feelings. Rather than take risks, we choose to hide, thereby eliminating the need to face an uncertain outcome.

When we isolate ourselves, we may:

Fearing rejection	Feeling defeated
Be loneliness	Be timid and shy
Procrastinate	See ourselves as different

Consider situations where isolation is a problem for you.

Example: **I isolate** from my spouse **because** he/she is so negative toward me. **This affects** my self-esteem. **This activates** my negative self-talk and anger. **This makes me feel** worthless and stupid.

Self-evaluation: On a scale from one to ten, how much does isolation negatively affect your life? Number one indicates that it has little negative effect. Number ten indicates that it has great negative effect. Circle where you are today.

| 1 | 2 | 3 | 4 | 5 | 6 | 7 | 8 | 9 | 10 |

LOW SELF-ESTEEM

Low self-esteem is rooted in our early childhood. During this time we were rarely encouraged to believe that we were adequate or important. Because of constant criticism, we believed that we were "bad" and the cause of many family problems. To feel accepted, we tried harder to please. The harder we tried, the more frustrated we became. Low self-esteem affects our ability to set and achieve goals. We are afraid to take risks. We feel responsible for things that go wrong, and when something goes right, we do not give ourselves credit. Instead, we feel undeserving and believe it is not going to last.

When we experience low self-esteem, we may:

Be non-assertive	Isolate from others
Fear failure	Have a negative self-image
Appear inadequate	Rescue or please others

Consider situations where low self-esteem is a problem for you.

Example: **I have low self-esteem** when I'm asked to speak in front of others **because** I believe everyone knows how worthless and unimportant I feel inside. **This affects** my ability to speak intelligently. I mumble, make excuses, and apologize for myself. **This activates** self-hatred and negative self-talk. **This makes me feel** hopeless.

Self-evaluation: On a scale from one to ten, how much does low self-esteem negatively affect your life? Number one indicates that it has little negative effect. Number ten indicates that it has great negative effect. Circle where you are today.

1	2	3	4	5	6	7	8	9	10

OVERDEVELOPED SENSE OF RESPONSIBILITY

As children in a dysfunctional home, we felt responsible for our parents' problems. We tried to be "model children" and arrange things the way we thought others wanted them to be. We believed that we were responsible for the emotions and actions of others—even for the outcome of events. Today we remain supersensitive to the needs of others, and we try to assume responsibility for helping them get their needs met. It is important for us to be perfect. We volunteer to do things so people will appreciate us. Our sense of responsibility causes us to overcommit, and we have a tendency to take on more than we can handle effectively.

When we are too responsible, we may:

Take life too seriously	Over-achieve
Appear rigid	Have false pride
Be perfectionists	Manipulate others

Consider situations where being over responsible is a problem for you.

Example: **I feel overly responsible** when things aren't going well at work **because** I feel as though it's my fault. **This affects** my health. I'm extremely tense and I get headaches. **This activates** my resentment and anger. I hate these people for letting me do all the work. **This makes me feel** guilty.

Self-evaluation: On a scale from one to ten, how much does overdeveloped sense of responsibility negatively affect your life? Number one indicates that it has little negative effect. Number ten indicates that it has great negative effect. Circle where you are today.

1	2	3	4	5	6	7	8	9	10

IRRESPONSIBILITY

In childhood, life was so chaotic we felt that nothing we did mattered. The models we had were untrustworthy and irresponsible, so we didn't know what was normal. The expectations placed on us were beyond our ability to achieve. We couldn't be what everyone wanted us to be, so we quit trying. Rather than compete with successful siblings, we unplugged, we gave up. As adults we are irresponsible. We wait for things to change before we begin to take initiative. We believe life has been so unfair to us that we won't claim responsibility for our condition. We are overwhelmed by our problems, but don't know how we can make a difference.

When we are irresponsible, we may:

Become detached	Under-achieve
Appear uncaring	Have false pride
Feel like victims	Expect others to take care of us

Consider situations where irresponsibility is a problem for you.

Example: **I feel irresponsible** when too much is expected of me **because** I know that I can't please my family. **This affects** my self-esteem. I want to isolate and hide. **This activates** my resentment and anger. I hate these people for expecting this of me. **This makes me feel** guilty and afraid.

Self-evaluation: On a scale from one to ten, how much does irresponsibility negatively affect your life? Number one indicates that it has little negative effect. Number ten indicates that it has great negative effect. Circle where you are today.

1	2	3	4	5	6	7	8	9	10

REPRESSED SEXUALITY

We find ourselves confused and uncertain about our sexual feelings toward others, particularly those close to us or those with whom we hope to be emotionally intimate. Because it is awkward to share our feelings with others, we have no opportunity to develop a healthy attitude about our own sexuality. As small children we may have heard the message "sex is dirty and not to be talked about." Some of us saw our parents as very disapproving or as totally nonsexual. We may have been molested by a parent or close relative who was out of control. As a result, we are uncomfortable in our sexual roles. We do not freely discuss sex with our partners for fear of being misunderstood or abandoned.

Due to repressed sexuality we may:

Feel guilt and shame   Lose our sense of morality
Be frigid or impotent   Avoid intimacy
Seduce others   Be lustful

Consider situations where your sexuality is a problem for you.

Example: **I repress my sexuality** when my spouse wants intimacy **because** I feel dirty and unlovable. **This affects** our relationship. **This activates** my resentment and anger toward my spouse for not understanding, consequently I hate myself for being this way. **This makes me feel** lonely.

Self-evaluation: On a scale from one to ten, how much does your repressed sexuality negatively affect your life? Number one indicates that it has little negative effect. Number ten indicates that it has great negative effect. Circle where you are today.

| 1 | 2 | 3 | 4 | 5 | 6 | 7 | 8 | 9 | 10 |

CHARACTER STRENGTHS

Consider the positive character strengths you already possess in the following areas:

Emotional: Healthy feelings or affective responses to one's self and others (e.g., I am able to feel and express my love for my spouse and my children).

Spiritual: The good ways one relates to God (e.g., I have a strong commitment to Jesus Christ).

Relational: Positive and supportive interaction with others (e.g., I have a healthy friendship with Robert).

Moral: Proper ethics and behavior in thoughts and actions (e.g., I have a clear conscience concerning my business affairs).

Intellectual: Quality attention and energy devoted to mental activities (e.g., I devote time to reading and study).

Self-care/nurturing: Healthy concern and care for self. (e.g., I take time to go fishing).

ADDITIONAL INVENTORY

Take time now to consider the weaknesses and strengths that you did not consider in your Step Four inventory.

STEP FIVE

Admitted to God, to ourselves, and to another human being the exact nature of our wrongs.

• • •

Therefore confess your sins to each other and pray for each other so that you may be healed.

(JAMES 5:16A)

Understanding Step Five

Imagine a house that had been shut up for several years. A blanket of dust covers everything. Signs of decay abound: cobwebs in strings like party decorations. Stuffy and stale odors of mildew and mold. Unrecognizable knickknacks on the dust-covered mantle. Forgotten and faded pictures on stained walls. Eerie feelings that hover like ghosts from years gone by. We can't wait to open all the doors, to pull back all the drapes, to vent the shut-up rooms. We turn on every light and expose each darkened, dusty corner. We watch the light of day sweep out the demons of darkness and shadow.

Our lives are like closed-up houses. All our shameful secrets, embarrassing behaviors, and spoiled hopes lie hidden from view. The air of our lives is stale because we have been afraid to open the doors and windows to anyone else lest we be found out, rejected, or shamed. Step Five is our emergence. When we admit the nature of our wrongs to God, ourselves, and another human being, we are opening the doors and windows of our lives. We are displaying our true selves.

Working Step Five

We work Step Five by bringing our Step Four inventory to God in prayerful admission. We work Step Five by being honest with ourselves, by looking ourselves in the eye, and reciting our inventory. We work Step Five by sharing our inventory with someone we can trust, someone who will understand, someone who will encourage and not condemn us.

Preparing for Step Five

We prepare for Step Five by scheduling an undistracted time with God and with ourselves. We prepare by prayerfully searching for another human being with whom to share. And we prepare by asking God for help in completing this step. Sometimes our tendency is to round off the edges and water down the truth of our inventory. God can give us the courage to be brutally honest about ourselves.

Prayer for Step Five

Higher Power,
My inventory has shown me who I am, yet I ask for your help in admitting my wrongs to another person and to you. Assure me, and be with me in this step, for without this step I cannot progress in my recovery. With your help, I can do this, and I will do it.

(Taken from *Prayers for The Twelve Steps—A Spiritual Journey*, page 16)

Step Four laid the foundation for identifying many of our shadowy deeds and thoughts. It also provided an opportunity for recording our strengths. Completing our Step Four inventory made us aware of many truths about ourselves. This realization may have caused us pain. The natural reaction is to feel sadness or guilt or both. We faced ourselves and our history honestly. We courageously identified some behaviors we want to eliminate.

For those of us who have been honest and thorough, Step Four has provided the foundation upon which we will build our recovery. It identified the unresolved feelings, unhealed memories, and personal defects that produced resentment, depression, and loss of self-worth. God's help and light (John 1:5–9) helped us commit our lives to walking in the light of his truth. The acknowledgment of our wrongs and the mending of our self-worth have begun to lift a great burden from our hearts and minds. Now that we have identified our character traits, it is possible to relieve ourselves of the burden of guilt and shame associated with our wrongdoings.

Step Five requires that we engage in honest confrontations with ourselves and others by admitting our faults to God, to ourselves, and to another person. By doing so, we begin the important phase of setting aside our pride so that we can see ourselves in true perspective.

Admitting the exact nature of our wrongs to God is the first phase of Step Five. Here, we confess to God all that we have worked so hard to conceal. It is no longer necessary to blame God or others for what has happened to us. We begin to accept our history for exactly what it is. This process of acceptance brings us closer to God, and we start to realize that he is always there for us. Our confession helps us receive God's love and accept ourselves unconditionally. We must remember that we are all children of God and will never be rejected.

Admitting our wrongs to ourselves began in Step Four, as we wrote our inventory and had the opportunity to see our behaviors for what they really are. In Step Five, we consciously admit our wrongs. This increases our self-esteem and supports us as we move toward Step Seven, in which we ask God to remove our shortcomings.

Telling our story to another person can be a frightening experience. Many of us have spent a major portion of our lives building defenses to keep others out. Living in isolation has been a way of protecting ourselves from further hurt. Step Five is our pathway out of isolation and loneliness, a move toward wholeness, happiness, and a sense of peace. It is a humbling experience to be totally honest, but we can no longer pretend. It is time to reveal ourselves completely to another human being.

We will unveil parts of our nature that we have concealed from ourselves. We may fear the impact that telling the truth will have on our lives. Sharing our story with another person may cause us additional fear of being rejected. However, it is essential that we take this important risk and confess our wrongs. With God's help, we will have the courage to reveal our true nature. The result will be worth all the agony of the unburdening process.

Following are some important guidelines to focus on when completing the Fifth Step:

- Remember that Step Five asks only that we admit the exact nature of our wrongs. We admit how our behaviors have been hurtful to ourselves and others. It is not necessary to discuss how the wrongs came about or how changes will be made. You are not seeking advice.

- Begin with prayer, calling upon God to be present as you prepare to go through your fourth step revelations and insights. Ask God's Spirit to guide and support you in what you are about to experience.

Helpful Hint: Read Step Five Prayers, page 16–17, *Prayers for The Twelve Steps—A Spiritual Journey.*

- Remember also to share your strengths. The objective is balance. Thank God for the strengths of character that he has nurtured in your life.

- After completing your fifth step, take time for prayer and meditation to reflect on what you have done. Thank God for the tools you have been given to improve your relationship with him. Spend time rereading the first five steps and note anything you have omitted. Acknowledge that you are laying a new foundation for your life. The cornerstone is your relationship with God and your commitment to honesty and humility.

- Congratulate yourself for having the courage to risk self-disclosure, and thank God for the peace of mind you have achieved.

Ask for God's help in choosing the person to whom you will admit your wrongs. Remember that the other person should reflect the image of Christ and be a representative for him. God intended us to speak to others, to share our sorrows and joys as members of his family. Look for qualities you admire in the other person that will inspire your confidence. Find someone on an equal spiritual level, with similar understanding. God's Holy Spirit works spiritually through all of his children. Sharing our personal experiences will help us come to know the depth of God's unconditional love for all his human family.

Choose your fifth step listener carefully, one who is familiar with Twelve-Step programs. The individual can be:

- A clergyman ordained by an established religion. Ministers of many faiths often receive such requests.

- A trusted friend (preferably of the same sex), a doctor, or psychologist.

- A family member with whom you can openly share. Be careful not to reveal information that might be harmful to your spouse or other family members.

- A member of a Twelve-Step program. If you are working with family groups as described in this book, you may find that significant trust already exists in your group. That trust will deepen by doing your fifth step with a group member. In some cases, the family group as a whole can be the listener.

- Choose a listener who is patient and sympathetic. The listener is God's spokesperson and is communicating God's unconditional acceptance.

- Choose a listener who is accepting and understanding.

LOOKING TO SCRIPTURE

Our growing relationship with God gave us the courage to examine ourselves, accept who we are, and reveal our true selves. Step Five helps us acknowledge and discard our old survival skills and move toward a new and healthier life. Being thorough and honest in completing our inventory places us in a position to face the facts and move forward.

> *Submit yourselves, then, to God. Resist the devil, and he will flee from you. Come near to God and he will come near to you. Wash your hands, you sinners, and purify your hearts, you double-minded.*
>
> JAMES 4:7–8
>
> • • •
>
> *Our personal inventory lets us acknowledge our past and turn with single-mindedness to the future.*

Helpful Hint: Read "Prayers of Penitence," Chapter Seven, page 93–103 *Prayers for The Twelve Steps—A Spiritual Journey.*

Step Five consists of three distinct parts. We will confess our faults to God, to ourselves, and to another human being. For some of us, it will involve telling our life story for the first time. As we do it, we will cleanse ourselves of the excess baggage we have been carrying. As we open our hearts and reveal ourselves, we will achieve a deeper level of spirituality. Self-disclosure is an important part of our spiritual life. We were created to live in community with both God and others. Living in community requires that we share ourselves and participate with others. Our self-defeating behaviors, as well as our shame, have caused us to isolate from others.

> *O Lord, we acknowledge our wickedness and the guilt of our fathers; we have indeed sinned against you.* JER. 14:20
>
> • • •
>
> *By focusing on God, we become aware of our desire to move away from the evil and toward the good.*

Admitting our defects to God can be very frightening. We may choose to believe that because God is in charge of the universe, all events are his will. In that way blaming God can be a method for us to deny our part in the problem. It is important to understand that God has given us free will. He wants what is best for us, but he allows us to make choices free of his manipulation. As we admit our wrongs to him, we must hold fast to his unconditional and everlasting love for us. He will strengthen and guide us, as we pursue his desire for us to lead a healthy and peaceful life.

> *So then, each of us will give an account of himself to God.*   ROM. 14:12
>
> • • •
>
> *Admitting our wrongs to God initiates the restoration of our personal integrity by removing the masks behind which we have hidden.*

Step Five is for your own benefit—God already knows you. You are beginning a process of living a life of humility, honesty, and courage. The result is freedom, happiness, and serenity.

The following information is helpful when completing your fifth step with God:

- Imagine God sitting across from you in a chair.

- Start with a prayer such as, "Lord, I understand that you already know me completely. I am now ready to reveal myself to you openly and humbly—my hurtful behaviors, self-centeredness, and negative traits. I am grateful to you for the gifts and abilities that have brought me to this point in my life. Take away my fear of being known and rejected. I place myself and my life in your care and keeping."

- Speak audibly, sincerely, and honestly. Share your understanding of the insights you gained from your fourth step inventory. Be aware that emotions may surface as part of the powerful cleansing experience taking place.

IF YOU HAVE NOT ALREADY DONE IT, STOP NOW AND
SHARE YOUR STEP FOUR INVENTORY WITH GOD.

Our admission to ourselves is the least-threatening part of Step Five and it can be done with the least risk. However, it is not the easiest part of Step Five because of denial.

We use denial as a coping mechanism—an unconscious tool to protect ourselves from pain. Through denial we are protected from facing the truth about ourselves. Denial is not easily conquered, but if we have done an honest Step Four inventory, the barrier of denial is already weakened.

> *If we claim to be without sin, we deceive ourselves and the truth is not in us. If we confess our sins, he is faithful and just and will forgive us our sins and purify us from all unrighteousness.*
>
> 1 JOHN 1:8–9
>
> • • •
>
> *Self-deception is human nature. In Step Five, we are challenged to be honest.*

Writing your fourth step inventory began the process of developing your self-awareness, This is the first step toward what will soon become genuine self-love. Solitary self-appraisal is the beginning of your confession. It is in Step Five that you turn that knowledge into improved self-acceptance.

The following information is helpful when completing your fifth step with yourself:

- Sit in a chair with your imaginary double seated across from you in an empty chair. Or sit in front of a mirror that allows you to see yourself as you speak.

- Speak out loud. Allow yourself time to hear what you are saying and to note any deeper understanding that occurs.

- Acknowledge your courage for proceeding to this point. This and every part of this process releases excess emotional baggage that you have carried around because of low self-worth and sense of shame.

IF YOU HAVE NOT ALREADY DONE IT, STOP NOW
AND SHARE YOUR STEP FOUR INVENTORY
WITH YOURSELF.

Admitting our wrongs to another human being is the most powerful part of Step Five. It is a true exercise in humility and will help us break down our defenses. Being rigorously honest with another human being may frighten us and cause us to procrastinate this portion of Step Five. It is tempting to believe that telling God is all that is necessary because he ultimately forgives all sins. While this is true, confession to another provides special healing and wholeness and releases the grip of hidden sin.

> *"When he came to his senses, he said, 'How many of my father's hired men have food to spare, and here I am starving to death! I will set out and go back to my father and say to him: Father, I have sinned against heaven and against you. I am no longer worthy to be called your son; make me like one of your hired men.' "* LUKE 15:17–19
>
> • • •
>
> *When we realize how far we have fallen, we clearly see the extent of our sin, perhaps for the first time.*

When choosing a person for Step Five, we will want to select a loving, caring person, one who will be there for us and who will provide unconditional acceptance. The person must be dependable, trustworthy, and not shocked or offended by what we reveal. It is wise to choose someone who is familiar with the program. Sharing will flow easily if there is honesty and opportunities for feedback from the other person. Trusting the person with whom we share our story is vital to the success of Step Five and will provide a safe atmosphere.

> *When I kept silent, my bones wasted away through my groaning all day long. For day and night your hand was heavy upon me; my strength was sapped as in the heat of summer...Then I acknowledged my sin to you and did not cover up my iniquity. I said, "I will confess my transgressions to the Lord"—and you forgave the guilt of my sin...*
>
> PS. 32:3–5
>
> • • •
>
> *Bearing the burden of our transgressions drains us of vital energy. Confession will renew our existence.*

Helpful Hint: Read Recovery Note for Psalm 32:5–9, *Life Recovery Bible.*

In telling our story to another person, we can expect more than just being heard. We must be ready to listen to the other person's response. The interchange can be helpful and productive if we are willing to listen with an open mind to the other person's viewpoint. This broadens our awareness of ourselves and gives us an opportunity to change and grow. Feedback is vital to us as a means of completing the process of revelation. Questions asked in a caring and understanding manner can reveal insights and feelings of which we are unaware.

Sharing our life story in this way can be one of the most important interactions in our lives. For this reason, we must watch for barriers we might unconsciously erect for protection. We should make eye contact, and consciously include the other person.

> *Therefore confess your sins to each other and pray for each other so that you may be healed. The prayer of a righteous man is powerful and effective.*
>
> JAMES 5:16
>
> • • •
>
> *Prayerful sharing with a brother or sister in Christ prepares the way for healing to begin.*

> *He who conceals his sins does not prosper, but whoever confesses and renounces them finds mercy.*
>
> PROV. 28:13
>
> • • •
>
> *In Step Five, we must relentlessly expose the exact nature of our wrongs, being always certain of God's merciful pardon.*

It takes considerable humility to bare ourselves to another person. We are about to reveal our self-defeating, damaging, and harmful character traits. We also will mention our positive strengths and worthwhile traits. We must do this to remove the masks we present to the world. It is a bold step toward eliminating our need for pretense and hiding.

The following information is helpful when completing your fifth step with another person:

- Allow ample time to complete each thought and stay focused on the subject. Refrain from unnecessary explanations.

- Eliminate distractions. Telephone calls, children, visitors, and extraneous noises must not disrupt your sharing.

- When Step Five is completed, both parties can share their feelings about the experience. It is now possible to extend to each other the love God extends to us through Christ.

- It is possible that you will not see your fifth step listener again. That's OK. It is your decision to continue the relationship in whatever direction you choose, from casual friendship to deeper spiritual companionship.

IF YOU HAVE NOT ALREADY DONE IT, STOP NOW
AND SHARE YOUR STEP FOUR INVENTORY
WITH ANOTHER HUMAN BEING.

When Step Five is completed, some expectations may remain unfulfilled. We need to understand that God's timing is not always our timing. God works in each one of us according to our own capacity to respond to him. We are not to submit to our anxiety; instead, we are to trust God. The real test of our Step Five admission is our willingness to trust that God will strengthen and develop our capacity to change our lives.

> *"If you have played the fool and exalted yourself, or if you have planned evil, clap your hand over your mouth!"* PROV. 30:32
>
> • • •
>
> *Acknowledging our lustful, prideful nature can be our first exercise in experiencing humility. We begin to understand how much God must love us.*

Upon completion of Step Five, we will realize that we are not always in control. It is not easy to change our old behavior patterns all at once. Admitting the exact nature of our wrongs is no guarantee we will stop acting in our old ways. We can expect to have moments of weakness. But we can also be strong in knowing that our relationship with God can help us overcome them. If we sincerely want to change our ways, God will give us the strength and courage required.

> *For all have sinned and fall short of the glory of God.* ROM. 3:23
>
> • • •
>
> *Our Step Five admissions help us realize how we have fallen short of God's plan for us.*

Helpful Hint: Read Meditation for Romans 3:23, page 72, *Meditations for The Twelve Steps—A Spiritual Journey.*

KEY IDEAS

Shadow: In Step Five we come to grips with our shadow. In Step Four we noted the presence of our shadow, but we really didn't confront how it impacted our life. It's like coming to believe that a mouse is at work in our kitchen during the night. In the mornings, we find droppings and teeth marks, but we don't see the mouse itself. In Step Four we noted the evidence and identified the problems, but in Step Five we catch the mouse. We admit to our wrongs openly.

Confession: In Step Five, confession is the act of admitting our wrongs. To confess is to acknowledge openly what we have discovered about ourselves in our Step Four inventory. In confession we speak the truth about ourselves; we tell our story. We end the silence, the isolation, the hiding.

*Were entirely ready to have God remove
all these defects of character.*

• • •

*Humble yourselves before the Lord,
and he will lift you up.*

(JAMES 4:10)

Understanding Step Six

When a farmer works a field, he begins with soil preparation. The farmer will plow, disc, harrow, fertilize, harrow again, and finally plant. For a period of time the farmer is visibly active in his field. But after he plants, he stops for a while to allow the new seeds to grow. There is nothing he can do except wait and hope.

In Step Six, activity ceases for a season. The seeds of change that God planted are allowed time to germinate and grow. Our emotions are allowed time to catch up with our new experiences. We have been plowed and prepared, and now we give God's power the necessary time to create in us an internal change.

Working Step Six

We work Step Six by being ready to have God bring change into our lives. Becoming ready doesn't seem like work, but it is—it's spiritual work. God can't change us unless we are willing for him to do so, and so far we have not asked God for change. We have only become aware of our condition and admitted our need. In future steps we will ask God to remove our shortcomings and to help us set things straight. In this step we wait for God to do some internal work, and we must be sensitive to the changes he is making in our hearts.

Preparing for Step Six

We prepare for Step Six by quieting our minds and opening our hearts. Steps Four and Five required a lot of hard work and brought up some painful discoveries about ourselves. Now we can best prepare for the next leg of the journey by making quiet time for ourselves. We put down the pencils and put on the walking shoes. Taking time to be alone with ourselves and with God helps us to remove the distractions that sometimes shield us from reality.

Prayer for Step Six

Dear God,
I am ready for your help in removing from me the defects of character that I now realize are an obstacle to my recovery. Help me to continue being honest with myself and guide me toward spiritual and mental health.

(Taken from *Prayers for The Twelve Steps—A Spiritual Journey,* page 18)

Having completed Steps One through Five, some of us may believe that we can stop here. The truth is much more work lies ahead. The best results are yet to come. In Steps One and Two, we recognized our powerlessness and came to believe in a power greater than ourselves. In Step Three, we turned our wills and our lives over to God's care. In Steps Four and Five we honestly faced the truth about ourselves and admitted that truth to God, to ourselves, and to another person. We may have an illusion that everything is OK and that the remaining steps are less important. If we believe this, we will surely undermine our progress.

Steps One through Five helped to steer us in the right direction as we built a foundation for ultimate surrender. In Step Six, we confront the need to change our attitudes and behaviors. Here, we prepare to make these changes and totally alter the course of our lives.

The changes that are about to take place in our lives require a cooperative effort. God provides the direction and plants the desire. We contribute the willingness to take the action required. Our job is to respond to God's leadership in our journey. God never forces himself on us. We must invite him into our lives. That is why Step Six is so important. This step provides us with the opportunity to become ready for God's deepest work, which is yet to come.

We are not expected to remove our character defects alone. We are expected only to let go and let God. Step Six is not an action step that we actually take. It is a state of preparation that enables us to become ready to release our faults to God. Our willingness to surrender will increase. This enables us to reach the point (in Step Seven) where we are ready to let God take over and remove our faults as he sees fit. We do this by working the program, one day at a time, regardless of whether or not we see any progress.

We must remind ourselves that the character traits we want to eliminate are often deeply ingrained patterns of behavior, developed through many years of struggling to survive. They will not vanish overnight. These self-defeating character traits are a part of us. They are the tools we used as a way of coping with our environment. For many of us, we could be identified by labels such as "the responsible one," "the angry one," or "the silent one." We must be patient while God is reshaping us. Through our new willingness to let God be in control, we learn to trust him more completely. This frees us to welcome his timetable for our growth.

Step Six is similar to Step Two. Both steps deal with our willingness to allow God to work through us to change our lives. In Step Two, we seek restoration to sanity by coming to believe in a power greater than ourselves. In Step Six, we seek readiness to let God remove our shortcomings. Both steps acknowledge the existence of problems and require that we seek God's help in being freed from them. The fact that we "came to believe" will strengthen our capacity to be "entirely ready."

LOOKING TO SCRIPTURE

To be successful with Step Six, we must sincerely want to change our disabling behaviors. But even this desire to change will come from God's grace as we wait upon his will for our lives. Our past has been dominated by our self-will, through which we sought to control our environment. We victimized ourselves by our self-will, rarely calling on God for help. Our life's condition shows us that self-will has never been enough to help us. Now, honest determination to eliminate our behavior flaws causes us to seek God's will. Before we can accept God's help, we must relinquish our self-destructive natures.

Therefore, prepare your minds for action; be self-controlled; set your hope fully on the grace to be given you when Jesus Christ is revealed.

1 PET. 1:13

• • •

Focusing on preparation for change will encourage our faith by allowing us to gracefully detach from our past.

Helpful Hint: Read Meditation for 1 Peter 1:13, page 76, *Meditations for The Twelve Steps—A Spiritual Journey.*

At this point in our program, we see that change is necessary to live life to the fullest. Recognizing the need for change and being willing to change are two different matters. The space between recognition and willingness to change can be filled with fear. As we move toward willingness, we must let go of our fears and remain secure in the knowledge that with God's guidance, everything will be restored to us.

This fear arises when we feel as though everything is our responsibility. Something inside our heads says, "God helps those who help themselves. So get busy and change!" Change comes from God, not from our self-will. And it comes when we are willing to let go.

Delight yourself in the Lord and he will give you the desires of your heart. Commit your way to the Lord; trust in him and he will do this. PS. 37:4–5

• • •

By learning to live in the light of God's love, we glimpse the new life that is possible for us.

> *Not that I have already obtained all this, or have already been made perfect, but I press on to take hold of that for which Christ Jesus took hold of me. Brothers, I do not consider myself yet to have taken hold of it. But one thing I do: Forgetting what is behind and straining toward what is ahead, I press on toward the goal to win the prize for which God has called me heavenward in Christ Jesus.*   PHIL. 3:12–14
>
> • • •
>
> *Forgetting the past and putting it behind us is an important element in our recovery.*

Our character defects are familiar tools to us. The loss of them threatens our ability to control ourselves and others. The thought of giving up our defects may cause anxiety, but God won't remove a character trait we need. When we place our trust in God we develop a sense of comfort. Even the smallest beginning is acceptable to God. Scripture tells us that if we have faith as small as a mustard seed nothing is impossible. When we have planted the seed of our willingness, we need to protect the tiny sprouts of positive results. We do not want the weeds of self-will to overrun our new garden. These seedlings of "willingness" respond quickly to our nurturing.

> *Do not conform any longer to the pattern of this world, but be transformed by the renewing of your mind. Then you will be able to test and approve what God's will is—his good, pleasing and perfect will.*   ROM. 12:2
>
> • • •
>
> *As our minds turn from things "of this world" to things "of God," our transformation begins.*

Our ability to talk to God is an important part of Step Six. We need to communicate with him in a way that shows our humility and invites his intervention. When we say, "Dear God, I want to be more patient," we are making a demand and telling God what we want. When we say "Dear God, I am impatient," we present the truth about ourselves. When we pray in this manner, we exhibit humility, relinquish our pride, and ask God to act on our behalf.

Helpful Hint: Read "Prayers of Petition" and "Prayers of Declaration," Chapters Two & Three, pages 35–65, *Prayers for The Twelve Steps—A Spiritual Journey.*

Humble yourselves before the Lord, and he will lift you up. JAMES 4:10

• • •

We demonstrate our humility by allowing God to lead us through our healing. Our guideline must be his way, not our way.

If any of you lacks wisdom, he should ask God, who gives generously to all without finding fault, and it will be given to him. But when he asks, he must believe and not doubt, because he who doubts is like a wave of the sea, blown and tossed by the wind. JAMES 1:5–6

• • •

Our doubts are overcome by our growing faith in what we know to be true—that God, our heavenly Father, will never forsake us.

This step requires that we look at the shortcomings we will ask to have removed. We may be unwilling to give up some of them. They may seem useful to us, so we respond, "I cannot give up...yet." We have a potential problem if we say "I will never be any different and will never give up." These attitudes shut our minds to God's redeeming qualities and can add to our own destruction. If we respond this way to any behavior, we need to admit our doubts and struggles to God and seek his help in surrendering to his will.

"BROKEN DREAMS"

As children bring their broken toys
with tears for us to mend,
I brought my broken dreams to God
because He was my friend.
But then, instead of leaving Him
in peace to work alone,
I hung around and tried to help
with ways that were my own.
At last, I snatched them back and cried,
"How can you be so slow?"
"My child," He said,
"What could I do?
"You never did let go."
–Author unknown

But the Lord is faithful, and he will strengthen and protect you from the evil one. 2 THES. 3:3

• • •

Chaos and confusion can occur when we experience changes in our lives. As we begin to rely on God's presence within us, our feelings of comfort and safety will overcome our anxiety.

As we follow the principles of the program in our daily lives, we gradually and unconsciously prepare to have our shortcomings removed. Sometimes, we are even unaware of our readiness to have our defects removed. At first, we realize that we are behaving differently—that we have changed. Sometimes, others note the changes before we become aware of them ourselves. Approval seekers begin to function more independently; control addicts become more easygoing and more relaxed; caretakers become more sensitive to their own needs. People who diligently work the program as an integral part of their lives become calmer, more serene, and genuinely happy.

> *In the same way, count yourselves dead to sin but alive to God in Christ Jesus. Therefore do not let sin reign in your mortal body so that you obey its evil desires.* ROM. 6:11–12
>
> • • •
>
> *Temptation's hold on us is shattered by our willingness to let Christ lead us to healthy behavior.*

Helpful Hint: Read Recovery Note for Romans 6:12–14, *Life Recovery Bible.*

A radiant, confident person lives in each of us, hidden under a cloud of confusion and uncertainty, distracted by ineffective behavior. The more we work the program and understand ourselves, the more we feel the weight and burden of our self-defeating behavior, and the more we long to change. If someone asked us if we wanted to be freed from our character defects, we could give only one answer—we are entirely ready to have God remove them.

> *I seek you with all my heart; do not let me stray from your commands. I have hidden your word in my heart that I might not sin against you. Praise be to you, O Lord; teach me your decrees.*
>
> PS. 119:10–12
>
> • • •
>
> *Centering our attention on the word of God enables us to receive his teaching and do his will.*

> **This is the assurance we have in approaching God: that is if we ask anything according to his will, he hears us. And if we know that he hears us— whatever we ask—we know that we have what we asked of him.** 1 JOHN 5:14–15
>
> • • •
>
> *As we come closer to God in our minds and in our lives, we soon trust that he will hear our prayers and heal us.*

KEY IDEAS

Readiness: Step Six is a time to overcome fear and gather the readiness we need to proceed with our recovery. We now know the truth about ourselves and what faults must be removed. In Step Six we need readiness and willingness to allow God to change us. This step is like bungee jumping. You may be dressed to jump, and have all the facts about the bungee cord. You may even have complete confidence in the operators, but you won't jump until you're ready. And you won't be ready until you overcome your fear. Your defects are a part of you. They have helped you survive. The thought of losing anything, even your damaging defects, tends to produce fear.

Defects of Character: Our defects of character are called many things in the program. They are called character weaknesses, faults, shortcomings, harmful behaviors, survival skills, negative traits, etc. Whatever the name, the point is the same. These undesirable parts of ourselves must be removed and replaced with godly character. These defects of character began innocently in childhood. They were our means of survival. We learned to manipulate in order to have our needs met, to lie to protect ourselves, and to hide our emotions in defense against overwhelming pain. In short, we learned how to survive. These survival skills were tools of control. They were our ways of managing our environment, minimizing our threats, and taking care of ourselves. Eventually, these coping skills break down. It is then we realize that God is the only one able and wise enough to control our lives.

Willingness: Willingness is a state of mind and emotions that propels us into action. We may have the best intentions, but until we are willing to act, we won't. There are many singles today who want to get married, who intend to get married, and who even know whom to marry, but they won't marry because they are not yet willing. In Step Six all of our good intentions simmer and brew until, with God's help, we are entirely ready and willing to change.

STEP SEVEN

***Humbly asked Him to remove
our shortcomings.***

• • •

*If we confess our sins, he is faithful and
just and will forgive us our sins and
purify us from all unrighteousness.*

(1 JOHN 1:9)

Understanding Step Seven

Anyone who has been seriously ill or injured knows what it's like to need others. It is indeed humbling when we are in that sickbed and unable to move or care for ourselves. Even the simplest of needs must be met by another. By the time we come to Step Seven we realize that we are on a sickbed, and the only one who can meet our needs is God. Every step, up till now, has reinforced the same theme: We are unable, but God is able. So now as we lie helpless and humbled on the sickbed of our disease, we pray: "Remove my shortcomings."

Working Step Seven

Step Seven requires prayer. We work this step on our knees. Our condition, our honesty, and our pain have humbled us so now we must open our mouths and pray. The temptation here is to pray a general prayer. We are tempted to ask God to remove everything as if it were a package deal. But that's not how the program works. If we were thorough, our Step Four inventory listed each character defect separately. Our confession in Step Five was also done item by item, and later our amends will be made individually. So now our Step Seven work is humble prayer for the removal of our shortcomings—one defect at a time.

Preparing for Step Seven

We prepare for Step Seven by holding nothing back from God—no glimmer of hope in our own ability to control. We prepare for Step Seven by making sure that we have overcome the fear of letting go of our defects. We prepare for Step Seven by learning to draw nearer to God, by becoming comfortable in God's presence.

Prayer for Step Seven

My Creator,
I am willing that you should have all of me, good and bad. I pray that you now remove from me every single defect of character that stands in the way of my usefulness to you and my fellows. Grant me strength as I go out from here to do your bidding.

(Taken from *Prayers for The Twelve Steps— A Spiritual Journey*, page 20)

Humility is a recurring theme in the Twelve-Step program and the central idea of Step Seven. By practicing humility we receive the grace necessary to work the program and achieve satisfactory results. We recognize now that most of our lives have been devoted to fulfilling our self-centered desires. We must set aside these prideful, less-than-nurturing behaviors, come to terms with our inadequacies, and realize that humbly seeking God's will alone will free our spirit. Step Seven requires surrendering our will to God so that we may receive the serenity necessary to achieve the happiness we seek.

We are growing in the wisdom and knowledge of Christ. This growth not only comes because we are seeking it, but also from the insight gained by examining the pain of our past struggles. We gain courage by hearing how others cope with their life challenges. As we work the steps, we recognize the value of acknowledging the truth of our past. Although the pain of this reality may seem unbearable, the insights we achieve are the only means to our release.

Step Six prepared us to let go of our old defective behaviors and freed us to develop the powerful new ones that God intends for us to use. Asking God to remove our faults is a true measure of our willingness to surrender control. For those of us who have spent our lives thinking we were self-sufficient, the surrender of control can be an extremely difficult task. Are we sincerely ready to abandon these deceptions? If so, then we can ask God to help us let go of our past and nurture the new life within us.

Step Seven is a vitally important part of the cleansing process and prepares us for the next stage of our journey. During the first six steps, we became aware of our problems, looked at our lives honestly, revealed previously hidden aspects of ourselves, and became ready to change our attitudes and behaviors. Step Seven presents us with the opportunity to turn to God and ask for removal of those parts of our character that cause us pain.

Before beginning this program, we avoided looking at ourselves honestly and admitting the extent of our disabling behavior. Meditating on the vision of Christ's presence in our lives will focus our attention on living life according to his example and begin to free us from this disabling burden of "self." Our partnership with Christ will increase our concern for the whole human family and put our obsession with "self" into its proper perspective. We will finally recognize the person we have been, understand who we are, and look forward with joy to the person we are becoming.

Preparing to have our shortcomings removed requires willingness to work with God to revise and redirect our attention and activity. Our progress will be halted if we continue our destructive behaviors. We must be ever-vigilant and alert to the possible return of "old behaviors" and work diligently toward eliminating them from our lives. It is wise to be gentle with ourselves and remember that it took us a lifetime to develop these habits. It is not realistic to expect them to disappear overnight.

When looking to God to remove our shortcomings, we do well to remember that God gives grace directly to us through prayer and meditation and also through other people. God often uses outside forces to correct our defects. Ministers, teachers, medical doctors, and therapists can all be instruments of God's grace. Our willingness to seek outside help can be a clear indication of our readiness to change. Compulsive worriers can pray to God to release their worries and, at the same time, seek help from a counselor to relieve their anxiety. Persons who overindulge in food or drugs can seek professional help to gain control over their obsessive habits. We need to pray for God's help in removing our shortcomings, and have the courage to seek appropriate professional help when we know we need it.

LOOKING TO SCRIPTURE

Through working the steps, we are progressing toward a happier and healthier life. We see how the opportunities and blessings that God brings into our lives surpass anything we could ever have created on our own. Having completed the first six steps, we are becoming aware of the multitude of benefits available to us. Through this awareness, we become grateful for God's presence and secure in the knowledge that our lives are improving.

> *Good and upright is the Lord; therefore he instructs sinners in his ways. He guides the humble in what is right and teaches them his way. All the ways of the Lord are loving and faithful for those who keep the demands of his covenant. For the sake of your name, O Lord, forgive my iniquity, though it is great.*   PS. 25:8–11
>
> • • •
>
> *As we work the steps and learn from God's work, we begin to see the gifts of God's grace being manifested in our lives.*

Step Seven implies that we ask for removal of all our shortcomings. However, the process will be more manageable if we deal with them individually, working on the easiest ones first to build up our confidence and strength. If we are patient, God will see that we achieve our goal at a pace that is comfortable for us. Our willingness to accept God's help builds trust and confidence in ourselves and in God. For now, use your Step Four inventory as your Step Seven guide to prayer. Remember that faith is required when you humbly ask God to remove your shortcomings. Trust that God hears and desires to answer, regardless of your emotions. You may not feel or experience any immediate change after you pray. Be confident, however, that God has heard your request and will work to remove your shortcomings.

> *Do not be anxious about anything, but in everything, by prayer and petition, with thanksgiving, present your requests to God.*　　　　PHIL. 4:6
>
> • • •
>
> *Through prayer and meditation, our anxieties are relieved and our faith is strengthened.*

We may find that after we ask God to relieve us of a burdensome behavior, it doesn't seem to go away. Becoming angry or discouraged is understandable but self-defeating. It is more productive to reach out and ask for prayer support from a friend in recovery. It helps to express our negative feelings to God in prayer, knowing that he understands. When things do not seem to go according to our timetable, reciting the Serenity Prayer can also work to our advantage.

> Helpful Hint: Read "Prayers of Complaint," Chapter Four, pages 67-75, *Prayers for The Twelve Steps—A Spiritual Journey.*

"PARADOXES OF PRAYER"

I asked God for strength, that I might achieve
I was made weak, that I might learn humbly to obey...
I asked for health, that I might do greater things
I was given infirmity, that I might do better things...
I asked for riches, that I might be happy

I was given poverty, that I might be wise...
I asked for power,
that I might have the praise of men
I was given weakness,
that I might feel the need of God...
I asked for all things, that I might enjoy life
I was given life, that I might enjoy all things...
I got nothing that I asked for—
but everything I had hoped for
Almost despite myself,
my unspoken prayers were answered
I am, among all, most richly blessed!
© Universal Press Syndicate

If we confess our sins, he is faithful and just and will forgive us our sins and purify us from all unrighteousness. 1 JOHN 1:9

. . .

Confession and forgiveness free us from the bondage and burdens of our past; all things are made new.

Letting go of negative behaviors, however destructive they are, may create a sense of loss and require that we allow ourselves time to grieve. It is normal to grieve for the loss of something we no longer have. In our childhood we may have experienced "things" being taken from us abruptly or before we were ready to release them. Now, we may be too sensitive and cling to "things" to avoid the pain of loss. So that we don't avoid or deny the existence of our fear of letting go, we can turn to our Lord for courage and trust the outcome to him. This is an opportunity to rely on our love and trust in God to heal our memories, repair the damage, and restore us to wholeness.

> *For whoever exalts himself will be hunbled, and whoever humbles himself will be exalted.*
>
> MATT.23:12
>
> • • •
>
> *Our recovery will be enhanced if we set aside our prideful self-will, and humbly ask God for guidance. A daily time for prayer and reflection is especially helpful.*

Helpful Hint: Read Meditation for Matthew 23:12, page 91, *Meditations for The Twelve Steps—A Spiritual Journey.*

Changing our behavior can be temporarily alarming to our sense of self. Our fear of not knowing what is ahead may cause us to repeat past destructive actions. We may retreat into feeling isolated and lose our sense of belonging. Having faith and trusting in our relationship with God shows our willingness to release the fear of being lost, frightened, or abandoned.

> *But he gives us more grace. That is why Scripture says: "God opposes the proud but gives grace to the humble." Submit yourselves, then, to God. Resist the devil, and he will flee from you. Come near to God and he will come near to you. Wash your hands, you sinners, and purify your hearts, you double-minded.*   JAMES 4:6–8
>
> • • •
>
> *Being submissive to God means seeking his presence, knowing his word, and doing his work.*

As we notice our defects being removed and our lives becoming less complicated, we must proceed with caution and guard against the temptation to be prideful. Sudden changes in our behavior can and do happen, but we cannot anticipate them or direct them. God initiates change when we are ready, and we cannot claim that we alone removed our character defects. When we learn to ask humbly for God's help in our lives, change becomes God's responsibility. We cannot accept the credit, but we can give thanks.

> *Create in me a pure heart, O God, and renew a steadfast spirit within me. Do not cast me from your presence or take your Holy Spirit from me. Restore to me the joy of your salvation and grant me a willing spirit, to sustain me.* PS. 51:10–12
>
> • • •
>
> *In periods of despair and doubt, we may feel separated from God. Being quiet and praying for guidance can restore our spirit and renew our trust.*

Destructive behaviors that remain after we complete Step Seven may never be eliminated, but we have an opportunity to transform these aspects of our character into positive traits and learn to use them in a constructive way. Leaders may be left with a quest for power but with no need to misuse it. Lovers will be left with exceptional sensuality but with enough sensitivity to refrain from causing pain to the person they love. Those who are materially wealthy may continue to have plenty but will set aside their greed and possessiveness. With the help of our Lord, all aspects of our personal lives can be rewarding. By continuing to practice humility and accept the tools God is giving us, we will eventually begin to aspire to a more Christlike life, sharing with others the love we have received. But none of this is accomplished through our own strength—it is God who is at work in our lives.

> *Humble yourselves, therefore, under God's mighty hand, that he may lift you up in due time. Cast all your anxiety on him because he cares for you.*
> 1 PETER 5:6–7
>
> • • •
>
> *As our fear lessens and we accept God's care and control, we begin to experience love and joy in our lives.*

For the program to be successful, we must practice the steps regularly. When we have moments of inner struggle, we can simply say, "This too will pass"; "I let go and let God"; "I fear no evil"; "I choose to see the good in this experience." These affirmations are useful to keep us from reverting to our obsessive/compulsive behaviors. Depression, guilt, and anger can be acknowledged and understood to be temporary reactions.

> *Have mercy on me, O God, according to your un-failing love; according to your great compassion blot out my transgressions. Wash away all my iniquity and cleanse me from my sin.* PS. 51:1–2
>
> • • •
>
> *When temptation and trial threaten our peace of mind, we call upon the Holy Spirit for assistance.*

We need to stop for a moment and acknowledge ourselves for our commitment to recovery. Note how determination enabled us to break the bonds of our unhealthy habits and behaviors. We can accept the positive, spontaneous thoughts and feelings that occur and see that this acceptance results from our personal relationship with God. We learn that the guidance we receive from our Lord is always available. All we need to do is listen, receive, and act without fear.

Helpful Hint: Read Serenity Prayer Devotional for Luke
11:37–44, *Life Recovery Bible.*

Repent, then, and turn to God, so that your sins may be wiped out, that times of refreshing may come from the Lord. ACTS 3:19

• • •

Step Seven has relieved us of the guilt and shame that shaped our lives for so long. Now our day of grace has come.

KEY IDEAS

Humility: Many of us in recovery misunderstand humility. If we are co-dependent, we might mistakenly think that humility is doing for others and placing ourselves second. If we tend toward manipulation, we might mistakenly think that our "poor me" performances are humility. Or we might think that simply saying "sorry" is a demonstration of humility. The truth is we don't know what healthy and godly humility is.

True biblical humility implies that we see ourselves as God sees us. It is putting ourself in proper perspective in light of God's plan. Appropriate humility is seen in Christ, who emptied himself to obey God's will, to serve others, and to fulfill God's plan for his life. Christ had every right to approach this world with superiority, but instead, he came as a lowly servant doing God's will. So we can be Christlike in our humility as we place ourselves under God's control and submit to his will and plan for our lives.

Understanding Step Eight

"Mom! Sarah hit me!" R. J. screamed like a siren.

"But he kicked me first," Sarah answered in defense.

"Yeah, but she took my game."

"He shouldn't be so touchy." And so it goes....

Does any of this sound familiar? Kids love to blame others for their troubles, and they hate to accept any responsibility. We adults might occasionally compel them to accept responsibility and coerce them into a forced apology. But they would never freely choose to say, "I'm sorry. My behavior was out of line."

In Step Eight we begin to grow up. We start doing what spiritually mature people can do—take responsibility for our actions without consideration for the wrongs done to us by others. Throughout these steps we have been dealing with our own stuff. Step Four was *our* moral inventory— nobody else's. Our Step Five admissions were for *our* wrongs. The shortcomings belong to *us*. In Step Eight, we continue to look at ourselves. But this time, we are considering those people who were harmed by our character defects.

Working Step Eight

We work Step Eight with thoughtful reflection. With God's help, we recall the names and faces of people we have harmed. Our job is to write their names down and consider each person carefully. We need to examine our relationship with these people and consider how we have harmed them. We will help ourselves by being as thorough as possible in our considerations and notes.

Preparing for Step Eight

We prepare for Step Eight through practicing humility. The willingness to be humble puts our lives in proper perspective and places us in agreement with God's plan and will for our lives. Step Eight requires that we recognize our part in the harm that has been done to others.

On a practical note, we prepare for Step Eight by making room in our lives for reflection. This may mean attending a retreat or setting aside some time to be quiet and thoughtful.

Prayer for Step Eight

Higher Power,
I ask your help in making a list all those I have harmed.
I will take responsibility for my mistakes, and be forgiving to others as you are forgiving to me. Grant me the willingness to begin my restitution. This I pray.

(Taken from *Prayers for The Twelve Steps—A Spiritual Journey*, page 22)

Before entering the Twelve-Step program, many of us blamed our parents, relatives, and friends for the turmoil in our lives. We even held God responsible. In Step Eight, we begin the process of releasing the need to blame others for our misfortune and accepting full responsibility for our own lives. Our Fourth Step inventory revealed that our inappropriate behavior caused injury not only to us but also to the significant others in our lives. Now we must prepare to accept full responsibility and make amends.

Steps One through Seven helped us to center ourselves in the healing power of Jesus Christ. His Holy Spirit started the process of getting our lives in order. We were given the tools to examine our personal experiences and to see the importance of letting go of the past. We were freed to continue our personal growth by facing our history and putting it behind us. That growth is related directly to our success in looking at and then releasing our history. Like barnacles on a ship's hull, our past wrongdoings can prevent us from sailing smoothly to a life filled with peace.

Working Steps Eight and Nine will improve our relationships, both with ourselves and others. These steps also invite us to leave behind our isolation and loneliness. The key factor here is our willingness to make amends to those we have harmed. As we continue to welcome Christ's presence into our hearts, we will develop a new openness with others. This openness will prepare us for the face-to-face amends to follow. In Step Eight, we examine each past misdeed and identify the persons involved. Our intention is to make amends and heal our past so that God can transform the present.

Reviewing our Fourth Step inventory will help us determine who belongs on our list. Making amends is a difficult task—one that we will execute with increasing skill, yet never really finish. Again, uncomfortable feelings may surface as we come to grips with our past behaviors. As we recognize the damage caused by our actions, we will realize what great relief awaits us when we no longer cause injury to ourselves and others.

For many of us, admitting our misdeeds will be difficult. The pattern of our lives has been to blame others and to seek retribution for the wrongs done to us. When we look at ourselves, we see that the retribution we vainly sought only created more havoc. By insisting on our own measure of justice, we lost the ability to set and achieve positive goals. Cycles of hatred and hard feelings were created, and we kept our attention focused away from our wrongs. These feelings will continue to prevent our growth so long as we continue to judge others and focus on their misdeeds. There is no doubt others have shortcomings, but our job is to focus on our own behaviors.

Forgiving ourselves and others helps us overcome our resentments. God has already forgiven us for the harmful actions that separated us from him. Developing the ability to forgive ourselves is an important element in our ongoing recovery. The ability to forgive others is essential. Amends without forgiveness leads to dishonesty and further complicates our lives.

To repair our past wrongdoings, we must be willing to face those wrongs by recording the harm we think we have caused. When preparing the list of people we have harmed, it is best to keep our thoughts directed toward making things right. Although our intentions may be rebuffed, our desire is to obey God and find healing. People on our list may feel bitter toward us and resist our attempts at restitution. They may hold deep grudges and be unwilling to reconcile with us. No matter how we are received, we must be willing to proceed with our amends. The amends we make are principally for our own benefit, not the benefit of those we have harmed.

Following are three main categories in which we may have caused harm and for which we must be willing to make amends.

Material Wrongs: Actions that affected an individual in a tangible way (e.g., borrowing or spending extravagance, stinginess, spending in an attempt to buy friendship or love, withholding money in order to gratify ourselves, entering agreements that are legally enforceable and refusing to abide by the terms, injuring or damaging persons or property because of our actions).

Moral Wrongs: Inappropriate behavior in moral or ethical actions and conduct, including questions of rightness, fairness, or equity (e.g., involving others in our wrongdoing, setting a bad example for children, friends, or anyone who looks to us for guidance, being preoccupied with selfish pursuits and totally unaware of the needs of others, forgetting birthdays, holidays, and other special occasions, sexual infidelity, broken promises, verbal abuse, lack of trust, lying).

Spiritual Wrongs: "Acts of omission" because of neglecting our obligations to God, to ourselves, to family, and to community (e.g., failure to make an effort to fulfill obligations, not showing gratitude toward others who have helped us, avoiding self-development in areas such as health, education, recreation, or creativity, being inattentive to others in our lives by failing to provide encouragement to them).

LOOKING TO SCRIPTURE

Step Eight begins the process of healing damaged relationships through our willingness to make amends for past misdeeds. We can let go of our resentments and start

to overcome the guilt, shame, and low self-esteem we have
found through our harmful actions. We can leave behind
the gray, angry world of loneliness and move toward a
bright future by exercising our new willingness to make
things right. Through the gifts of God's work and the steps,
we have the necessary tools to overcome past wreckage
and mend our broken relationships.

> *But Zacchaeus stood up and said to the Lord, "Look,
> Lord! Here and now I give half of my possessions
> to the poor, and if I have cheated anybody out of
> anything, I will pay back four times the amount."*
>
> LUKE 19:8
>
> • • •
>
> *As we identify those we have harmed, we also must
> prepare to make restitution.*

Helpful Hint: Read Meditation for Luke 19:8, page 100,
Meditations for The Twelve Steps—A Spiritual Journey.

As Christians, we are taught the importance of having and
maintaining deep, loving relationships. Through Christ's example, we see how he devoted his ministry to loving people
and encouraging them to love one another. Christ taught
that being reconciled to God requires reconciliation with
other human beings.

> *Dear friends, since God so loved us, we also ought
> to love one another. No one has ever seen God;
> but if we love one another, God lives in us and
> his love is made complete in us.*   1 JOHN 4:11–12
>
> • • •
>
> *Our willingness to make amends gives us an opportunity
> to love one another and experience how God lives in us.*

In Step Eight, we prepare ourselves to continue work on God's plan for our lives by becoming willing to make amends. Once we have prepared our list of those we have harmed, we then begin to ask God for the willingness needed to make the amends. With God's help we will be able to extend love and acceptance to the injured persons.

> *For if you forgive men when they sin against you, your heavenly Father will also forgive you. But if you do not forgive men their sins, your Father will not forgive your sins.* MATT. 6:14–15
>
> • • •
>
> *Withholding our forgiveness inhibits our spiritual growth and perpetuates the continuance of guilt and shame.*

Forgiveness is a two-way street. As Christ declared in the Lord's Prayer: "Forgive us our trespasses, as we forgive those who trespass against us...." We need to ask forgiveness of those we have harmed. And we need to forgive those who have harmed us. As we reflect on our Lord, we see how he encourages us to turn the other cheek, to love our enemies, and to pray for our persecutors. Only in this manner can we break the cycle of hatred and violence. None of this is possible if we rely on our own strength. God knows how we struggle with these things, and he awaits our honest cry for help.

> *You...have no excuse, you who pass judgment on someone else, for at whatever point you judge the other, you are condemning yourself, because you who pass judgment do the same things.* ROM. 2:1
>
> • • •
>
> *Passing judgment on others removes us from God's grace and condemns us to repeat the pain of the past.*

> *"But I tell you who hear me: Love your enemies, do good to those who hate you, bless those who curse you, pray for those who mistreat you. If someone strikes you on one cheek, turn to him the other also...Give to everyone who asks you, and if anyone takes what belongs to you, do not demand it back. Do to others as you would have them do to you."*
>
> LUKE 6: 27–31
>
> • • •
>
> *Our healing will be noticeable to us when we are willing, even eager, to return good for evil.*

When making our list, we need to examine our relationships with people at home and in our community. If we ask God to help us, our task will be much easier. We can ask him for guidance in selecting the names of the persons with whom we need to communicate. If we set aside our pride, we will see that the thoughts and feelings of others have worth and value. We do not have to agree with everyone, nor must they agree with us. But we can stop disliking people for what they think and do. We can stop resenting them because their views are different from ours. Remember that Christ encourages us to love even our enemies and thereby be like our heavenly Father.

> *"Do not judge, and you will not be judged. Do not condemn, and you will not be condemned. Forgive, and you will be forgiven. Give, and it will be given to you. A good measure...will be poured into your lap. For with the measure you use, it will be measured to you."* LUKE 6:37–38
>
> • • •
>
> *Receiving the gift of God's love and freely giving it to others assures an abundant life for us.*

> Helpful Hint: Read "Prayers of Intercession," Chapter Nine, pp. 115–125, *Prayers for The Twelve Steps—A Spiritual Journey.*

Occasionally we will be prevented from facing the people on our list directly. They may be deceased, separated from us, or unwilling to meet with us. Whatever the situation, we still need to put them on our list. When we make the amends in Step Nine, we will see why amends are necessary, even if they cannot be made face-to-face. Being willing to make the amends will release us from hard feelings and enable us to experience serenity and peace of mind. When making our Step Eight list, we shouldn't exclude any portion, any period, or any person from our list. With God's help, we can include any name that comes to mind.

> *Be kind and compassionate to one another, forgiving each other, just as in Christ God forgave you.*   EPH. 4:32
>
> • • •
>
> *Step Eight involves replacing bad feelings with compassion for ourselves and all of God's human family.*

When looking at those persons we have harmed, we see how our character defects have played a major part in sabotaging our lives and our relationships. For example:

- When we became angry, we often harmed ourselves more than others. This may have resulted in feelings of depression or self-pity.

- Persistent financial problems resulting from our irresponsible actions caused difficulty with our family and creditors.

- When confronted with issues about which we felt guilty, we lashed out at others instead of looking honestly at ourselves.

- Frustrated by our lack of control, we behaved aggressively and intimidated those around us.

- Because of our indiscriminate sexual behavior, true intimacy was impossible to achieve or maintain.

- Our fear of abandonment sometimes destroyed our relationships because we did not allow others to be themselves. We created dependency and attempted to control their behavior by trying to maintain the relationship we wanted.

> *We who are strong ought to bear with the failings of the weak and not to please ourselves. Each of us should please his neighbor for his good, to build him up. For even Christ did not please himself, but, as it is written: "The insults of those who insult you have fallen on me."* ROM. 15:1–3
>
> • • •
>
> *As we grow in spiritual strength, we become willing servants of God, caring for our neighbors as God cares for us.*

Helpful Hint: Read Recovery Note for Romans 15:1–6, *Life Recovery Bible.*

When making a list of people for our amends, we need to remember to focus on ourselves. Many of us were victims of self-inflicted pain because we did not have the skills to take care of ourselves appropriately. We spent time and energy trying to be available for everybody and sacrificed ourselves in the process. We may have been our own worst enemy and experienced excessive self-blame, guilt, and shame. Taking time to look at the harm we have inflicted upon ourselves and being willing to forgive ourselves is essential to our continued growth.

> *"Why do you look at the speck of sawdust in your brother's eye and pay no attention to the plank in your own eye? How can you say to your brother, 'Let me take the speck out of your eye,' when all the time there is a plank in your own eye?"*
>
> MATT. 7:3–4
>
> • • •
>
> *Honest self-appraisal is a daily necessity if we are to be restored to wholeness. Vigilant appraisal of our thoughts and habits must become routine.*

In Step Nine, we seek out the people we have harmed and make amends wherever necessary. For now, all we need to do is list them and describe the harmful behavior. The consequences of our actions may have produced emotional, financial, or physical pain to others. We need to take as much time as necessary to reflect on our list and be as thorough as possible. Being totally honest with ourselves is a major factor in our ability to make restitution for our past destructive actions. During this process, blaming, finding excuses, and rationalization can obscure our ability to be honest. Therefore, we should pay special attention to the names that cause us difficulty.

> *"And when you stand praying, if you hold anything against anyone, forgive him, so that your Father in heaven may forgive you your sins."*
>
> MARK 11:25
>
> • • •
>
> *God's promise of healing cannot be fulfilled if we refuse to relinquish our anger and resentment. Our success in working Step Eight will depend directly on our ability to forgive.*

KEY IDEAS

Amends: Within the context of the Twelve-Step program, the idea of amends is broadly defined as "repairing the damage of the past." Amends can be as simple as an apology or as complex as restitution for physical or financial liability.

Forgiveness: Forgiveness is a key part of Step Eight. When we work this step and begin to make a list of the persons we have harmed, we immediately think about how others have harmed us. Perhaps this reaction is a defense mechanism—a way to avoid admitting guilt. It doesn't matter why we feel this way; what matters is that we deal with it. We need to forgive those who have hurt us—our forgiveness, according to Scripture, depends on it.

Forgiveness is not an emotion. It is a decision. Forgiveness can only be real with God's help. God alone can give us the grace, desire, and ability to release those who have hurt us. Left to ourselves, we allow unforgiveness, bitterness, and resentment to fester.

AMENDS LIST

Person	Relationship	My Wrong-doing	Effects on Others	Effects on Me
Joan	wife	angry insults	fear, anger	guilt, shame
John	coworker	sexual advances	distrust, shame	loss of self-respect

STEP NINE

Made direct amends to such people wherever possible, except when to do so would injure them or others.

• • •

Therefore, if you are offering your gift at the altar and there remember that your brother has something against you, leave your gift there in front of the altar. First go and be reconciled to your brother; then come and offer your gift.

(MATT. 5:23–24)

Understanding Step Nine

Natural disasters are always gripping news. Earthquakes, hurricanes, forest or brush fires, and floods capture our attention. But rarely do we see the hard work of rebuilding that takes place after the disaster has past. Lives, homes, businesses, and whole communities are repaired and revived.

Step Nine is similar to the repairs and rebuilding that take place after a disaster. Through the process of making amends, we begin to mend the damage of our past. In Step Eight we surveyed the damage and made a plan. Now, in Step Nine, we go into action.

Working Step Nine

Working Step Nine involves personal contacts with those we have harmed. We go down our Step Eight list person by person. We approach each one with gentleness, sensitivity, and understanding. God can help us to know the best way to make contact. Some people will require a face-to-face meeting, while other situations may be handled by changing our behavior. Whatever the case, God provides us with the wisdom and direction we need.

Preparing for Step Nine

We prepare for Step Nine by making our Step Eight list as complete as possible and by being willing to make the amends. As we pray over every name, God will give us special insight and direction. He will also help us overcome the fear and apprehension that crops us.

Prayer for Step Nine

Higher Power,

I pray for the right attitude to make my amends, being ever mindful not to harm others in the process. I ask for your guidance in making indirect amends. Most important, I will continue to make amends by staying abstinent, helping others, and growing in spiritual progress.

(Taken from *Prayers for The Twelve Steps—A Spiritual Journey*, page 24)

Step Nine completes the forgiveness process that began in Step Four and fulfills our requirement to reconcile with others. In this step, we clear our garden of the dead leaves—we rake up and discard the old habits. We are ready to face our faults, to admit the degree of our wrongs, and to ask for and extend forgiveness. Accepting responsibility for the harm done can be a humbling experience because it forces us to admit the effect we have had on others.

Since we began our recovery, we have come a long way toward developing a new lifestyle. We have seen how the powerlessness and unmanageability of our lives caused havoc. Our commitment to face our character flaws, to admit them to others, and, finally, to ask God for their removal, has been a humbling experience. In Steps Eight and Nine, we proceed with the final stage of cooperating with God in rebuilding our character.

The qualities we need to work Step Nine are available from God. He can give us the judgment and careful sense of timing, courage, and stamina we need. As we become more courageous, it will be easier and safer to talk honestly about our past behavior and admit to others that we have caused them harm.

Making amends helps release us from many of the resentments of our past. We achieve serenity in our lives by seeking forgiveness from those we have harmed and by making restitution where necessary. Without forgiveness, the resentments will continue to undermine our growth. Making amends releases us from guilt and promotes freedom and health in mind and body.

Some people in our lives feel bitter toward us. Others feel threatened by us and resent our changed behavior. We can pray about these people and ask that Christ's wisdom be made known to us. God gives us the discernment to consider the appropriateness of facing these people directly.

If we are to forgive ourselves completely, we must first acknowledge the pain that others have endured because of our actions. We can only pray that God will prepare their hearts to receive our amends.

Some stumbling blocks appear in Step Nine. We may procrastinate by telling ourselves "the time is not yet right." We may delay by finding excuses to avoid facing those we have harmed. We must be honest with ourselves and not procrastinate because of fear. Courage is an important requirement for the successful completion of this step. The very spirit of Step Nine is contained in our readiness to accept the consequences of our past.

Another delaying tactic is the temptation to let bygones be bygones. We rationalize that our past is behind us, that there is no need to stir up more trouble. We fantasize that amends for past misdeeds are unnecessary, that all we have to do is alter our current behavior. It is true that some of our past behaviors may be laid to rest without direct confrontation. Being supported by others during this leg of our journey enables us to face the people and issues on our amends list. Our improved life filled with peace and serenity is closely connected to confronting the fears and resentments of our past.

LOOKING TO SCRIPTURE

In order to complete Step Nine, we need to review our list from Step Eight and decide on the appropriate method to make each amend. Most situations will require direct contact, although some may be handled by simply changing our behavior. Whichever alternative we choose, it is important that the process of making amends be as complete as possible. As long as we are willing, God will direct our amends process.

> *We love because he first loved us. If anyone says, "I love God," yet hates his brother, he is a liar. For anyone who does not love his brother, whom he has seen, cannot love God, whom he has not seen.* 1 JOHN 4:19–21
>
> • • •
>
> *If we love God, we cannot hate any of his creation. A measure of our love for him is visible when we give this love to others.*

Helpful Hint: Read Step Nine Devotional on "Making Peace" from Matt. 5:23–25, *Life Recovery Bible.*

Step Nine has two distinct parts regarding making amends:

"Made Direct Amends to Such People Wherever Possible"

We make direct amends to people who are readily accessible and who can be approached when we are ready. These people may include family members, creditors, coworkers, and others to whom we owe an amend. They can be friends or enemies. As part of making the amend, we must try to repair to the best of our ability the damage that has been done. The other person's response may be surprising to us, especially if our amend is accepted. We may wonder why we waited so long to resolve the conflict. It would be rewarding to have a positive and healing encounter, but our amend is not dependent upon the other person's response. Our amend can be successful even if we are not well received.

> *"You have heard that it was said, 'Love your neigh-*
> *bor and hate your enemy.' But I tell you: Love*
> *your enemies and pray for those who persecute*
> *you."*   MATT. 5:43–44
>
> • • •
>
> *When we extend love to our enemies, we diminish their*
> *power over us and offer God's forgiveness, which he*
> *has so graciously given to us.*

There are situations that prevent us from making direct personal contact. These may involve people who are no longer accessible or who are deceased. In these cases, indirect amends can satisfy our need for reconciliation. These amends are accomplished through prayer or by writing a letter, as if we were communicating with the absent person. Another way to make amends to such a person is to ask a close friend to sit in the place of the inaccessible person to whom we need to make the amend. We then speak with the close friend as if we were speaking to the other person directly. We also can make amends by performing a kindness for someone we may not even know, but who is connected in some way to the person we have harmed.

> *Above all, love each other deeply, because love cov-*
> *ers over a multitude of sins. Offer hospitality to*
> *one another without grumbling. Each one should*
> *use whatever gift he has received to serve others,*
> *faithfully administering God's grace in its various*
> *forms.*   1 PET. 4:8–10
>
> • • •
>
> *The fellowship of persons in a program of recovery*
> *offers an excellent opportunity to more fully understand*
> *what it means to be God's willing servant.*

"Except When to Do So Would Injure Them or Others"

Step Nine provides for those people to whom we can make only partial restitution because complete disclosure could cause harm to them or others. These people may include spouses, ex-partners, former business associates, or friends. We must analyze the harm they would suffer if complete disclosure was made. This is especially true in cases of infidelity. In such situations, irreparable damage could occur to all parties. Even if the matter must be discussed, we should avoid bringing harm to third parties. Amends for infidelity can be made by concentrating sincere affection and attention on persons to whom we have made loving commitments.

> *Therefore, if you are offering your gift at the altar and there remember that your brother has something against you, leave your gift there in front of the altar. First go and be reconciled to your brother; then come and offer your gift.*
>
> MATT. 5:23–24
>
> • • •
>
> *Clearing our lives of the damage caused by our past actions may appear insurmountable in the beginning of our program. Nevertheless, our commitment is to confront our resistance to doing God's will.*

There are situations where amends could result in serious consequences. In cases involving potential loss of employment, imprisonment, or alienation from one's family, we need to weigh the consequences carefully. If we delay our amends merely out of fear for ourselves or others, we will ultimately be the ones to suffer. In these situations, we can seek outside guidance from a counselor, minister, or close friend to decide how to proceed. Otherwise, we will delay our growth, and also experience stagnation in our progress toward building a new and healthier life.

> *...if he gives back what he took in pledge for a loan, returns what he has stolen, follows the decrees that give life, and does no evil, he will surely live; he will not die. None of the sins he has committed will be remembered against him. He has done what is just and right; he will surely live.*
>
> EZEK. 33:15–16
>
> • • •
>
> *Regardless of our motive for taking something that is not ours, keeping it only ensures our continued bondage to those things that keep us from the truth.*

There are amends that require deferred action. It is wise to seek counsel in situations where deferred action is required. It is seldom advisable to abruptly approach an individual who still suffers deeply from the injustices we have done. In situations where our own pain is still deeply imbedded, patience might be the wise choice. Timing is important. Our ultimate goals are personal growth and reconciliation. Recklessness and haste might create further injury and frustrate our ultimate goals.

> **Therefore encourage one another and build each other up, just as in fact you are doing.**
>
> 1 THESS. 5:11
>
> • • •
>
> *Looking only for the good in each other and ourselves enables us to avoid any destructive thoughts that could impair our relationships.*

Therefore let us stop passing judgment on one another. Instead, make up your mind not to put any stumbling block or obstacle in your brother's way.
ROM. 14:13

• • •

Judging others separates us from them and prevents us from extending the love to one another that God commands.

As we have learned, certain situations require special consideration. It is not our intention to cause additional harm in order to satisfy our need to make the amend. It is better to proceed slowly and be complete with the amend, rather than hurry and cause more damage. Here, God can be a great source of aid and comfort. We need to be constantly aware that his presence is with us now and will continue to be with us on our journey. Others may not understand or support our amend, but God stands ready to help see us through this process. God can provide us with a sense of his presence in our hearts and our minds.

"But love your enemies, do good to them, and lend to them without expecting to get anything back. Then your reward will be great, and you will be sons of the Most High, because he is kind to the ungrateful and wicked." LUKE 6:35–36

• • •

We receive God's grace without having to earn it. We must offer goodness to others in the same manner, expecting nothing in return.

To help in making the amend, first pray, then prepare a schedule listing the persons to contact, what you will say, how you will say it, and when you will say it. Writing letters and making phone calls are acceptable ways of making amends if face-to-face contact is not possible. Sometimes, meeting in person may not be the most desirable approach. The important thing is to make the amend before it is too late. Successful amends making will improve our relationship with those we have harmed and promote better relationships with others.

> *Let no debt remain outstanding, except the continuing debt to love one another, for he who loves his fellowman has fulfilled the law.*   ROM. 13:8
>
> • • •
>
> *Careful examination of our relationships with others will sometimes reveal forgotten debts. Keeping God's law requires that we make restitution.*

Helpful Hint: Read Meditation for Romans 13:8, page 122, *Meditations for The Twelve Steps—A Spiritual Journey.*

When working this step, we need to distinguish between amends and apologies. Apologies are appropriate; however, they are not substitutes for making amends. A person can apologize for being late for work, but until the behavior is corrected, an amend cannot be made. It is important to apologize when necessary, but it is more important to commit to changing the unacceptable behavior.

> *Do not repay anyone evil for evil. Be careful to do what is right in the eyes of everybody. If it is possible, as far as it depends on you, live at peace with everyone.*   ROM. 12:17–18
>
> • • •
>
> *Seeking revenge only perpetuates distress and frustration. God requires that we return good for evil.*

Occasional emotional or spiritual relapses are to be expected and should be dealt with promptly. If not, they will block our ability to make successful amends. When these relapses occur, we must accept them as signals that we are not working the program effectively. Perhaps we have turned away from God by not praying or reading Scripture daily and we need to return to Step Three. We may have eliminated something from our inventory and need to return to Step Four. Or we may be unwilling to relinquish a self-defeating behavior and need to return to Step Six.

> *Do nothing out of selfish ambition or vain conceit, but in humility consider others better than yourselves. Each of you should look not only to your own interests, but also to the interests of others.*
>
> PHIL. 2:3–4
>
> . . .
>
> *When we inflict harm on another, we cause harm to ourselves. Our program of recovery enhances our self-esteem and enables us to love and value others above ourselves, often looking out for their best interest before our own.*

Steps Eight and Nine help us repair the past. Through these steps, we take responsibility for causing injury to others and make restitution where necessary. We have a chance to redeem ourselves for past misdeeds by making amends, and we can look forward to a healthy and rewarding future life. We are now able to rebuild our self-esteem, achieve peaceful relations with ourselves and others, and live in harmony with our own personal world and with God.

Helpful Hint: Read "Finish the Business," page 24–25, *Prayers for The Twelve Steps—A Spiritual Journey.*

KEY IDEAS

Direct Amends: Direct amends are those amends that we make personally to someone we have harmed. We schedule appointments or plan to meet personally with them. If physical distance is a problem, we can call them on the phone or write a letter. The amend includes sharing with them that we are in a program that requires us to make amends. We request permission to make our amends to them; then we share our amend without blaming them or others. (See the **Amends to Others Guidelines** on page 153)

Indirect Amends: Indirect amends are nonpersonal amends that we make to those we have harmed. These include amends to someone who is deceased, whose location is unknown, or who is inaccessible for another reason. We can make indirect amends to these people through letters that are not mailed, through prayer to God, or by doing a kindness to someone else such as a family member of the person we have harmed.

Amends to Self: The one person we have often harmed the most is ourself. The amends process would not be complete without taking time to set things right with ourselves. The best way to accomplish this is to write a letter of amends to ourselves and then read it while sitting in front of a mirror. (See **Amends to Self Guidelines** on page 154)

AMENDS TO OTHERS GUIDELINES

This is a summary of ideas and procedures that have been useful in preparing for and making the amends in Step Nine. To align yourself with God's will, ask God to give you the correct attitude of heart so that you will be able to do the following.

Attitude

- Be willing to love and forgive yourself and the person to whom an amend is to be made.
- Know what you want to say and be careful not to blame the person with whom you are communicating.
- Take responsibility for what you are going to say.
- Be willing to accept the consequences.
- Resist the desire for a specific response from the other person.
- Be willing to turn your anxieties over to God.

Preparation

- Devote time to prayer and meditation.
- elay the amend if you are angry or upset and do more Step Four inventory work.
- Keep it simple. Details and explanations aren't necessary.
- Remember that the amend does not focus on the other person's part in the situation.
- Express your desire or ask permission to make the amend. For example: I am involved in a program that requires me to be aware of the harm I have done to others and to take responsibility for my actions. I'd like to make amends to you. Are you willing to receive them?

Sample Amends

- "I was _____ (scared, overwhelmed, feeling abandoned, etc.) when _____ happened between us. I ask your forgiveness for _____ (harm done) and for anything else I may have done in the past through my thoughts, words, or actions to cause you pain. I ask your forgiveness and assure you of my intention to change and to extend goodwill to you."

- "I want to make an amend to you about _____. For all those words that were said out of _____ (fear, thoughtlessness, etc.) and confusion, I ask your forgiveness. I extend my promise of love and caring toward you."

AMENDS TO SELF GUIDELINES

The following are some guidelines to use when making amends to yourself.

Attitude

- Be willing to love and forgive yourself.
- Know what you want to say and take responsibility for your actions.
- Have reasonable expectations of yourself.
- Be willing to turn your anxieties over to God.

Preparation

- Devote time to prayer and meditation.
- Delay the amend if you are angry or upset.
- Keep it simple. Explanations are not necessary.
- Remember the amend is to yourself and does not pertain to others.

Sample Amends

- "I was _____ (scared, overwhelmed, feeling abandoned, etc.) when _____ happened. I forgive myself for the _____ (harm done) and anything else I may have done in the past through my thoughts, words, or actions to cause myself harm."

- "I want to make an amend to myself about _____. I forgive myself for all the words that I said out of _____ (fear, thoughtlessness, etc.) and confusion."

STEP TEN

Continued to take personal inventory and, when we were wrong, promptly admitted it.

· · ·

So, if you think you are standing firm, be careful that you don't fall.

(1 COR. 10:12)

Understanding Step Ten

Anyone who has planted a garden knows the care required to keep it healthy. We must remove the rocks and the weeds, enrich the soil with fertilizer, bank it to hold water, plant the seeds, water, and guard against insects. Constant care is required to keep the garden clear of weeds, which could retake the garden if allowed. The garden once belonged to those weeds, and they always seem to want it back.

Our recovery is similar to a garden. Our lives once belonged to the weeds—our self-defeating behavior—but God has helped us plant a garden in our lives. He has pulled the weeds and caused some wonderful things to grow in their place. God used the steps as tools and raised us to a place where things are different. We are beginning to see the promise of fruit, the promise of lasting change. In the midst of this new garden, we can also see the return of weeds. They don't die easily. In fact, as long as we live, weeds—our old self-defeating ways—will seek to recapture our lives. For that reason we must be ever vigilant to work Step Ten. We must continue to take personal inventory and protect our garden.

Working Step Ten

Step Ten is really a routine summary of Steps Four through Nine. We take an inventory of our lives and admit what we find. We become willing to have God change us, and then we humbly ask God to remove the shortcomings. We make note of the amends needed and make those amends. The new element in Step Ten is the periodic inventory. We need to set aside regular times for personal inventory.

Preparing for Step Ten

We best prepare for Step Ten by scheduling time for our inventory. We might plan for our inventory by setting aside a portion of our daily devotional or journal time. An option is allowing time during lunch or just before bedtime. A more extensive inventory can be made by spending a weekend at a retreat center each quarter or twice a year. Whatever the interval of time, the key is committing to take a regular inventory.

Prayer for Step Ten

I pray I may continue:
To grow in understanding and effectiveness;
To take daily spot check inventories of myself;
To correct mistakes when I make them;
To take responsibility for my actions;
To be ever aware of my negative and self-defeating
    attitudes and behaviors;
To keep my willfulness in check;
To always remember I need your help;
To keep love and tolerance of other as my code; and
To continue in daily prayer how I can best serve you,
    my Higher Power.

(Taken from *Prayers for The Twelve Steps—A Spiritual Journey,* page 26)

In Step Ten, we begin the maintenance part of the steps. We will learn how to sustain what we have accomplished, become more confident, and proceed with joy along our spiritual journey. The first nine steps put our house in order and enabled us to change some of our destructive behaviors. This journey requires that we continue to rely on God's Holy Spirit and the inspiration of his word. Our work is beginning to pay off when we increase our capacity to develop new and healthier ways of taking care of ourselves and relating to others.

Some of us may wonder if the peace and serenity we are experiencing in our lives is permanent or just temporary. Working the steps has helped us see how fragile and vulnerable we are. But with daily practice of the steps and with Christ's loving presence in our lives, we will be able to achieve and maintain our newfound balance. Our relating skills will improve, and we will see how our interactions with others assume a new quality.

At this point, we may be tempted to revert to our old bravado and believe we are healed. We may think we have all the answers and can stop here. We feel comfortable with ourselves and see no need to continue with the program. We allow other activities to interfere and find excuses for skipping meetings and abandoning the program. We must resist this temptation to quit and realize that giving in will deprive us of realizing the goal we set for ourselves. Our successes can be maintained only if we are willing to depend upon God and practice the principles of the steps daily for the rest of our lives.

Step Ten points the way toward continued spiritual growth. In the past, we were constantly burdened by the results of our inattention to what we were doing. We allowed small problems to become large by ignoring them until they multiplied. Through our lack of sensitivity and skills to improve our behavior, we allowed our ineffective behavior to create havoc in our lives. In Step Ten, we consciously examine our daily conduct and confess our wrongs where necessary. We look at ourselves, see our errors, promptly admit them, and seek God's guidance in correcting them. While we are working so carefully to monitor our actions and reactions, we must not judge ourselves too harshly. We need to recognize that nurturing ourselves emotionally and spiritually requires daily vigilance, loving understanding, and patience. Life is never static; it is constantly changing, and each change requires adjustment and growth.

A personal inventory is a daily examination of our strengths and weaknesses, motives and behaviors. It is as important as prayer and Bible study in nurturing our ongoing spiritual growth. Taking daily inventory is not a time-consuming task and can usually be accomplished within fifteen minutes. When done with discipline and regularity, this is a small price to pay for continuing the good work we have begun.

It's important to monitor ourselves for signs that we are returning to old ways. We may be attempting to manage our lives alone, or slipping into old patterns of resentment, dishonesty, or selfishness. When we see these temptations arising, we must immediately ask God to forgive us, then make amends where needed. Daily practice of Step Ten maintains our honesty and humility and allows us to continue our development.

We become more conscious of our strengths and weaknesses when we take regular inventory. We are less inclined to yield to feelings of anger, loneliness, and self-righteousness when we are emotionally balanced, and when we know that we will hold ourselves accountable for our attitudes and behaviors. Our personal inventory helps us discover who we are, what we are, and where we are going. We become more focused and better prepared to live the Christian life we desire.

LOOKING TO SCRIPTURE

The program emphasizes regular personal inventory because many of us haven't developed the basic tools for self-appraisal. In time, we will appreciate the value of personal inventory. Although Step Ten inventories require some time and energy, the results are worth the effort. Three types of inventories are recommended; each serves a different purpose. These are *Spot-Check Inventory, Daily Inventory,* and *Long-Term Periodic Inventory.*

> *Whoever of you loves life and desires to see many good days, keep your tongue from evil and your lips from speaking lies. Turn from evil and do good; seek peace and pursue it.* PS. 34:12–14
>
> • • •
>
> *Working the steps trains us to be sensitive to our behavior and encourages us to seek God's will for us. As we become more adept, we turn naturally from evil and toward God.*

Helpful Hint: Read "Prayers of Imprecation," Chapter Eight, pages 105–113, *Prayers for The Twelve Steps—A Spiritual Journey.*

Spot-Check Inventory

A spot-check inventory involves stopping several times each day to assess our behavior and attitude. It is a short review of our actions, thoughts, and motives. This review can be useful in calming stormy emotions and it keeps us in touch with our behavior. It is a chance for examining situations, seeing where we are wrong, and taking prompt corrective action. Taking frequent inventories and immediately admitting our wrongs keeps us free from guilt and supports our spiritual growth. It is a good way to keep our lives free from anger, resentment, and unforgiveness.

> *For by the grace given me I say to every one of you: Do not think of yourself more highly than you ought, but rather think of yourself with sober judgment, in accordance with the measure of faith God has given you.* ROM. 12:13
>
> • • •
>
> *Our continuing honest assessment of ourselves will become more finely tuned as more truth is revealed to us. We should view each new discovery with compassion and have faith that God will give us strength according to our needs.*

Daily Inventory

It is important to stop at the end of each day or start at the beginning of the next and review what has happened. This reminds us that the program is lived one day at a time and keeps us focused on the present.

> *"Settle matters quickly with your adversary who is taking you to court. Do it while you are still with him on the way, or he may hand you over to the judge, and the judge may hand you over to the officer, and you may be thrown into prison. I tell you the truth, you will not get out until you have paid the last penny."* MATT. 5:25–26
>
> • • •
>
> *In the past, our pride often prevented us from making timely settlements. Living in the light of God's love helps us correct our wrongs and forgive the faults of others.*

The daily inventory can be viewed as a balance sheet for the day—a summary of the good and the bad. It is an opportunity to reflect on our interactions with other people and review the way we responded to various situations that arose during the day. In the situations where we did well, we can feel good about ourselves and acknowledge our progress. In those situations where we tried and failed, we need to acknowledge our attempt because we *did* make an effort. We can then make amends and move forward with peace of mind. As we work the program, we can be assured that our number of successes will continue to increase.

> *Therefore each of you must put off falsehood and speak truthfully to his neighbor, for we are all members of one body. "In your anger do not sin": Do not let the sun go down while you are still angry, and do not give the devil a foothold. He who has been stealing must steal no longer, but must work, doing something useful with his own hands, that he may have something to share with those in need.*   EPH. 4:25–28
>
> • • •
>
> Delaying the resolution of angry feelings can cause physical, emotional, and spiritual damage. God's grace is sufficient to relinquish any hold that negativity may have on us.

Future situations may arise that will challenge our integrity and commitment. We need to be as honest and clear about our intentions as possible. Things to consider are:

- If we are slipping back, trying to control and manipulate others, we need to recognize this and ask God to correct it.

- If we are comparing ourselves to others and feeling inferior, we need to reach out to supportive friends. We can then honestly examine our feelings to renew our own sense of self-worth.

- If we are becoming obsessive or compulsive and not taking care of ourselves, we need to stop and ask our Higher Power for help. We need to decide what unmet needs we are trying to fulfill and understand how to meet these needs.

- If we are fearing authority figures, we need to find the reason for our fear, acknowledge it, and ask our Higher Power for help.

- If we are depressed, we need to discover the central issue causing us to feel withdrawn or sorry for ourselves.

- If we are repressing our feelings, we need to take the necessary risks and express our feelings assertively.

- If we are feeling anxious, we need to examine the reason and take the steps necessary to address the issue.

> *Anyone who listens to the word but does not do what it says is like a man who looks at his face in a mirror and, after looking at himself, goes away and immediately forgets what he looks like. But the man who looks intently into the perfect law that gives freedom, and continues to do this, not forgetting what he has heard, but doing it—he will be blessed in what he does.* JAMES 1:23–25
>
> • • •
>
> *The work we do in the Twelve-Step program provides a structure wherein we can look at ourselves with honesty and lovingly accept who we are.*

Helpful Hint: Read Devotional on "Looking in the Mirror" from James 1:21–25, *Life Recovery Bible.*

Long-Term Periodic Inventory

A long-term periodic inventory can be accomplished by being alone or going away for a time. These are special days that can be set aside for reflection on our lives. We might attend a retreat, take a short vacation, or simply find a place of solitude. This is an important time that provides an opportunity for us to renew our intention to live healthier and more fulfilling lives.

> **Therefore, if anyone is in Christ, he is a new creation; the old has gone, the new has come!**
>
> 2 COR. 5:17
>
> • • •
>
> *The renewal of our relationship with Christ has brought us new life. Through his love for us, our progress in recovery will be sustained.*

This inventory can be done once or twice a year and will give us a chance to reflect on our progress from a clearer perspective. We will have an opportunity to see the remarkable changes we have made and to renew our hope and courage. We must be careful not to inflate our ego and must remind ourselves that our progress is a product of God's help and careful spiritual growth.

Long-term inventories help us recognize problem areas and patterns in our lives. These inventories enable us to get a larger perspective of our behavior and allow us the chance to make significant changes. We will discover new defects as well as new strengths and have an opportunity to evaluate our relationship with God. We must remember that our relationship with our Higher Power is the foundation of our recovery. Our continued commitment to turn our lives over to God's care is a vital part of this continuing process of recovery.

> *You were taught, with regard to your former way of life, to put off your old self, which is being corrupted by its deceitful desires; to be made new in the attitude of your minds; and to put on the new self, created to be like God in true righteousness and holiness.* EPH. 4:22–24
>
> • • •
>
> *The steps repeatedly remind us that God is in charge, and that our new state of mind is grounded in what God wants for us, rather than in what we want for ourselves.*

If we sincerely want to change our lifestyle, we take personal inventory regularly and continue to interact with others in recovery. This reminds us that we are not unique— that everyone gets upset occasionally and no one is always "right." Through this awareness, we develop the ability to be forgiving and understanding. By being kind, courteous, and fair, we will often receive the same in return and can expect to achieve harmony in many of our relationships. As we progress in our recovery, we see how pointless it is to become angry or to allow others to inflict emotional pain on us. Taking periodic, regular inventory and promptly admitting our wrongs keeps us from harboring resentments and allows us to maintain respect for ourselves and others.

> *A patient man has great understanding, but a quick-tempered man displays folly. A heart at peace gives life to the body, but envy rots the bones.*
>
> PROV. 14:29–30
>
> • • •
>
> *A peaceful nature enables us to be compassionate and frees the mind and spirit to seek a quality life.*

The practice of Step Ten has many benefits; most importantly, it strengthens and protects our recovery. Step It us from returning to old behaviors such as:

- Medicating any discomfort through alcohol or drugs
- Distracting ourselves through compulsive behaviors such as eating or shopping
- Hiding from life through isolation
- Denying our needs through control and manipulation of others
- Escaping reality through fantasies
- Soothing our low self-esteem through people pleasing

> *So, if you think you are standing firm, be careful that you don't fall!*   1 COR. 10:12
>
> • • •
>
> *As we complete Step Ten, we must not be overconfident in our recovery. Slipping into past behaviors can endanger our commitment to do God's will.*

Helpful Hint: Read Meditation for 1 Corinthians 10:12, page 136, *Meditations for The Twelve Steps—A Spiritual Journey.*

Working the steps is a way for us to develop a daily discipline that deepens our love for God and enables us to be genuinely sorry for our wrongs. It helps us in continually striving for improvement in our relationships with God and others. Learning to face our faults daily and correct them promptly provides God with the opportunity to mold our character and lifestyle. Delay in admitting our wrongs shows a resistance to working Step Ten. This is harmful and will only make matters worse.

The practice of Step Ten has many rewards, such as:

- Diminishing relationship problems.
- Admitting our wrongs and no longer pretending we are flawless.
- Developing a better understanding of others and expressing ourselves honestly.

> *Be very careful, then, how you live—not as unwise but as wise, making the most of every opportunity, because the days are evil.*   EPH. 5:15–16
>
> • • •
>
> *Our peace and serenity will be strengthened by the ongoing Step work we do. We now know that each day is a new opportunity to actively protect and sustain our ongoing recovery.*

KEY IDEAS

Personal Inventory: The Step Ten personal inventory is much like the moral inventory in Step Four. The difference is the ongoing and frequent nature of the Step Ten inventory. The idea of "personal" is a reminder to us that the inventory process is about us, not others.

Spot-Check Inventory: The spot-check inventory is the most frequent self-check. Through this inventory we monitor our actions throughout the day. We might designate objects or times in our day as reminders. For example, a red dot on our desk calendar might serve as a reminder to take a spot-check inventory. Or a prayer taped to our refrigerator might help us remember.

Daily Inventory: Quality time everyday needs to be set aside for our daily inventory. This can be a few minutes before bed or early in the morning when our minds are clear. It is best to use a journal or inventory log for this daily inventory. This will serve as a reminder that progress is being made—one day at a time.

Long-Term Periodic Inventory: The long-term periodic inventory is done after a longer period of time. We may take this inventory every quarter, twice a year, or annually—the specific interval is not important. The idea is to occasionally get away and take a thorough inventory that reflects upon longer periods of time. In this way we are able to view patterns and seasons in our lives. If possible, it is helpful to find some form of retreat or solitude for this inventory.

IMPORTANT GUIDELINES IN EVALUATING PERSONAL GROWTH

The material offered in this guide is intended to help you evaluate your personal growth. It includes feelings and behaviors from the Step Four inventory exercise. They are presented again to provide you with the opportunity to evaluate your progress in these important areas.

When doing this inventory, choose traits, feelings, or behaviors that specifically apply to you. Don't tackle them all at once. Use recent events and record words and actions as accurately as possible. This process enables you to evaluate your growth. You are the primary beneficiary of your honesty and thoroughness in this inventory.

At the end of each character trait, feeling, or behavior is a "Self-Evaluation" exercise. This same exercise was used in Step Four. It is provided again as another opportunity to measure your growth.

RECOVERY FROM RESENTMENT

We experience a release from resentment when we begin to understand that those who mistreated us were also spiritually sick. We extend to them the tolerance and forgiveness that God gives us. When we concentrate on our own inventories in Steps Four and Ten, we put the wrongs of others out of our mind, and we focus on our faults, not the faults of others.

As we recover from resentment, we begin to:

Feel tolerance for others	Forgive those who hurt us
Focus on our inventory	Release the need to retaliate
Accept some blame	Feel compassion for others

Consider specific examples of your behavior that show you are overcoming resentment.

Self-evaluation: On a scale from one to ten, how much does resentment negatively affect your life? Number one indicates that it has little negative effect. Number ten indicates that it has great negative effect. Circle where you are today.

1	2	3	4	5	6	7	8	9	10

RECOVERY FROM FEAR

Fear becomes less of a problem for us as our faith in God grows. We list our fears one by one and consider why they have power over us. We especially note the fears that grow out of our failed self-reliance. God is able to manage where we could not. Our faith empowers us to release our need for self-reliance and the fear that goes with it.

As we recover from fear, we begin to:

Feel less threatened	Embrace change
Rely on God	Face our fear honestly
Feel more joy	Pray more

Consider specific examples of your behavior that show you are trusting God where you once feared.

Self-evaluation: On a scale from one to ten, how much does fear negatively affect your life? Number one indicates that it has little negative effect. Number ten indicates that it has great negative effect. Circle where you are today.

1	2	3	4	5	6	7	8	9	10

RECOVERY FROM INAPPROPRIATE ANGER

Learning to express anger appropriately is a major step in our recovery. It releases many hidden emotions and allows healing to take place. Expressing anger lets others know our limits and helps us to be honest with ourselves. As we learn to express anger more appropriately, we are better able to cope with our own hostility and also the anger of others. Our relationships improve as we begin to feel comfortable expressing ourselves. Stress-related problems diminish, and we even feel better physically.

As we recover from inappropriate anger, we begin to:

Express anger	Set limits for ourselves
Identify hurt feelings	Reduce stress and anxiety
Make reasonable requests	Enjoy inner peace

Consider specific examples of your behavior that show you can express anger in a healthy way.

Self-evaluation: On a scale from one to ten, how much does inappropriate anger negatively affect your life? Number one indicates that it has little negative effect. Number ten indicates that it has great negative effect. Circle where you are today.

1	2	3	4	5	6	7	8	9	10

RECOVERY FROM APPROVAL SEEKING

As we begin to rely on our own approval and that of our Higher Power, we understand that wanting approval is OK, and we learn to ask for it and not manipulate others to get it. We accept compliments from others and learn to simply say "thank you," believing that the compliment is sincere. We say "yes" when it is a comfortable answer. We are willing to say "no" when "no" is appropriate.

As we recover from inappropriate approval seeking, we begin to:

Recognize our own needs	Be loyal to oneself
Tell the truth about how we feel	Build our confidence

Consider specific examples of your behavior that show you have experienced some recovery from inappropriate approval seeking.

Self-evaluation: On a scale from one to ten, how much does approval seeking negatively affect your life? Number one indicates that it has little negative effect. Number ten indicates that it has great negative effect. Circle where you are today.

1	2	3	4	5	6	7	8	9	10

RECOVERY FROM CARETAKING

As we put aside the role of caretaker, we assume less responsibility for everyone and everything and we allow individuals to find their own way. We give them over to the care of their Higher Power, which is the best source for their guidance, love, and support. By dropping the burden of meeting everyone's needs, we find time to develop our own personalities. Our obsession with caring for others is replaced by an acceptance of the fact that ultimately we have no power over the lives of others. We realize that our main responsibility in life is for our own welfare and happiness. We turn other people over to God's care.

When we stop being caretakers, we begin to:

Stop rescuing others
Take care of ourselves

Develop our own identity
Recognize dependent
relationships

Consider specific examples of your behavior that show you are lessening your role as caretaker.

Self-evaluation: On a scale from one to ten, how much does caretaking negatively affect your life? Number one indicates that it has little negative effect. Number ten indicates that it has great negative effecte. Circle where you are today.

| 1 | 2 | 3 | 4 | 5 | 6 | 7 | 8 | 9 | 10 |

RECOVERY FROM CONTROL

As we become more aware of the way we have attempted to control people and things, we begin to realize that our efforts have been useless. We did not control anything or anyone except ourselves. We discover more effective ways to get our needs met when we start accepting God as the source of our security. As we begin to surrender our wills and our lives to his care, we will experience less stress and anxiety. We become more able to participate in activities without being primarily concerned with the outcome. Saying the Serenity Prayer is helpful whenever we begin to recognize the reappearance of our need for control.

As we learn to give up control, we begin to:

Accept change	Reduce our stress levels
Trust in ourselves	Find ways to have fun
Empower others	Accept others as they are

Consider specific examples of your behavior that show you feel less of a need to be in control.

Self-evaluation: On a scale from one to ten, how much does controlling negatively affect your life? Number one indicates that it has little negative effect. Number ten indicates that it has great negative effect. Circle where you are today.

| 1 | 2 | 3 | 4 | 5 | 6 | 7 | 8 | 9 | 10 |

RECOVERY FROM FEAR
OF ABANDONMENT

As we learn to rely more upon the ever-present love of God, our confidence in life and the future increases. Our fear of abandonment diminishes and is replaced by the feeling that we are worthy people in our own right. We seek out healthy relationships with people who love and take care of themselves. We feel more secure in revealing our feelings. We transfer our old dependence on others to trust in God. We learn to understand and accept a nurturing and loving fellowship within our community. Our self-confidence grows as we begin to realize that with God in our lives, we will never again be totally alone.

As fear of abandonment diminishes, we begin to:

Be honest about feelings

Consider our own needs
   in a relationship

Reduce our caretaking

Feel comfortable
   being alone

Consider specific examples of your behavior that show your fear of abandonment is decreasing.

Self-evaluation: On a scale from one to ten, how much does fear of abandonment negatively affect your life? Number one indicates that it has little negative effect. Number ten indicates that it has great negative effect. Circle where you are today.

1	2	3	4	5	6	7	8	9	10

RECOVERY FROM FEAR
OF AUTHORITY FIGURES

As we begin to feel comfortable with people in roles of authority, we learn to put our focus on ourselves and discover that we have nothing to fear. We recognize others to be like us, with their own fears, defenses, and insecurities. Others' behavior no longer dictates how we feel about ourselves. We start acting and not reacting when responding to others. We recognize that our ultimate authority figure is God and that he is always with us.

As we become comfortable with authority figures, we begin to:

Act with increased self-esteem   Experience less fear
Accept constructive criticism   Interact easily with
Stand up for ourselves   people in authority

Consider specific examples of your behavior that show you are gaining confidence around people in authority.

Self-evaluation: On a scale from one to ten, how much does fear of authority figures negatively affect your life? Number one indicates that it has little negative effect. Number ten indicates that it has great negative effect. Circle where you are today.

| 1 | 2 | 3 | 4 | 5 | 6 | 7 | 8 | 9 | 10 |

RECOVERY FROM FROZEN FEELINGS

As we get in touch with our feelings and learn to express them, strange things begin to happen. Our stress levels decrease as we become able to express ourselves honestly, and we begin to see ourselves as worthy. We learn that expression of true feelings is the healthy way to communicate, and we find that more of our own needs are being met. All we have to do is ask. As we begin to release our feelings, we experience some levels of pain. But, as our courage increases, the pain goes away, and we develop a sense of peace and serenity. The more willing we are to take risks in releasing our emotions, the more effective our recovery will be.

As we experience and express our feelings, we begin to:

Feel free to cry	Experience our true self
Feel healthier	Express our needs to others

Consider specific examples of your behavior that show you are becoming aware of your feelings and are able to express them more easily.

Self-evaluation: On a scale from one to ten, how much do frozen feelings negatively affect your life? Number one indicates that they have little negative effect. Number ten indicates that they have great negative effect. Circle where you are today.

1	2	3	4	5	6	7	8	9	10

RECOVERY FROM ISOLATION

As we begin to feel better about ourselves, we become more willing to take risks and expose ourselves to new surroundings. We seek friends and relationships that are nurturing, safe, and supportive. We learn to participate and to have fun in group activities. It becomes easier to express our feelings as we develop a stronger sense of self-esteem. We recognize that people will accept us for who we really are. Our self-acceptance allows us to experience the precious gift of living more comfortably and serenely.

As we isolate less often, we begin to:

Accept ourselves

Freely express our emotions

Actively participate with others

Complete projects

Cultivate supportive relationships

Consider specific examples of your behavior that show you isolate yourself less frequently.

Self-evaluation: On a scale from one to ten, how much does isolation negatively affect your life? Number one indicates that it has little negative effect. Number ten indicates that it has great negative effect. Circle where you are today.

| 1 | 2 | 3 | 4 | 5 | 6 | 7 | 8 | 9 | 10 |

RECOVERY FROM LOW SELF-ESTEEM

As we work with our Higher Power to build confidence in ourselves and our abilities, our self-esteem increases. We are able to interact with others and accept ourselves as we really are. We see our strengths as well as our limitations. We learn to accept ourselves at face value. We become more willing to take risks, and we realize we can achieve many things that we had never dreamed possible. Sharing feelings with others becomes more comfortable. We feel safer as we come to know others and allow them to know us. Relationships become healthier because we are able to trust and validate ourselves. We no longer need to look to others for validation.

As our self-esteem increases, we begin to:

Be more confident	Love ourselves
Act more assertively	Openly express feelings
Easily interact with others	Take risks

Consider specific examples of your behavior that show your self-esteem is improving.

Self-evaluation: On a scale from one to ten, how much does low self-esteem negatively affect your life? Number one indicates that it has little negative effect. Number ten indicates that it has great negative effect. Circle where you are today.

| 1 | 2 | 3 | 4 | 5 | 6 | 7 | 8 | 9 | 10 |

RECOVERY FROM OVERDEVELOPED SENSE OF RESPONSIBILITY

Accepting the fact that we are not responsible for the actions and feelings of others forces us to focus on ourselves. We understand that we cannot force others to change and that people are responsible for themselves. As we assume responsibility for our own actions, we become aware that we must rely on God for guidance and take care of our own needs. Then we will find time and energy to support and nurture ourselves.

As we stop being too responsible, we begin to:

Take care of ourselves   Accept our limitations
Enjoy leisure time   Delegate responsibility

Consider specific examples of your behavior that show you are feeling less responsible for others.

Self-evaluation: On a scale from one to ten, how much does overdeveloped sense of responsibility negatively affect your life? Number one indicates that it has little negative effect. Number ten indicates that it has great negative effect. Circle where you are today.

| 1 | 2 | 3 | 4 | 5 | 6 | 7 | 8 | 9 | 10 |

RECOVERY FROM IRRESPONSIBILITY

As we understand that God will help us achieve realistic goals, we begin to work in partnership with God for our future. We place less value on the expectations others have of us and more value on our own desires to achieve goals in life. We understand that we are competing only with ourselves, and God will enable us to do what is needed to win at life. God brings order to our lives as we give him control, and he makes it possible for us to contribute in meaningful ways.

As we recover from irresponsibility, we begin to:

Keep commitments
Set goals for ourselves

Accept responsibilities
Feel better about ourselves

Consider specific examples of your behavior that show you are less irresponsible.

Self-evaluation: On a scale from one to ten, how much does irresponsibility negatively affect your life? Number one indicates that it has little negative effect. Number ten indicates that it has great negative effect. Circle where you are today.

| 1 | 2 | 3 | 4 | 5 | 6 | 7 | 8 | 9 | 10 |

RECOVERY FROM REPRESSED SEXUALITY

As we rely upon the constant love of our Lord, our self-worth increases, and we see ourselves as worthy in his eyes and in the eyes of others. As we increase our self-love and our ability to take care of ourselves, we seek to be with other healthy people who love and take care of themselves. We fear commitment less and are better prepared to enter a healthy relationship—emotionally, intellectually, and sexually. We feel more secure in sharing our feelings, strengths, and weaknesses. Our self-confidence grows and allows us to be vulnerable. We give up the need for perfection in ourselves and others and, in so doing, open ourselves to growth and change. We are honest about our own sexuality with our children. We accept their need for information and also their need for a healthy sexual identity.

When we accept our sexuality, we begin to:

Discuss sex openly   Share intimate feelings
Accept our sexual self   Consider our own
                                 sexual needs

Consider specific examples of how you are becoming comfortable with your sexuality.

Self-evaluation: On a scale from one to ten, how much does repressed sexuality negatively affect your life? Number one indicates that it has little negative effect. Number ten indicates that it has great negative effect. Circle where you are today.

| 1 | 2 | 3 | 4 | 5 | 6 | 7 | 8 | 9 | 10 |

Understanding Step Eleven

Vital to a healthy relationship is honest communication. If partners choose not to talk with each other, their relationship will suffer in every area and eventually will fail. On the other hand, when communication exists, relationships are strengthened, and broken relationships can be healed and restored.

Our relationship with God is our most important relationship. And relationship with God is impossible without communication. As we draw nearer to God in prayer and meditation, we draw closer to our source of power, serenity, guidance, and healing. To ignore communication with God is to unplug our power source.

Working Step Eleven

We work Step Eleven through the practice of prayer and meditation. Through prayer we talk to God and through meditation we listen to him. Many of us, however, struggle with prayer. We know prayers, but we don't know how to pray. Step Eleven is communicating with God. It is the process of learning the intimacy and power of prayer and meditation. It is the act of drawing near God.

Preparing for Step Eleven

We prepare for Step Eleven by taking prayer and meditation seriously. There is a tendency to put prayer and meditation on the second shelf, to treat both as nonimportant. We need to prepare for this step by developing an appreciation for prayer and meditation. If we struggle in this area, we might counsel with a minister, talk with an experienced program member, or otherwise seek help and insight.

Prayer for Step Eleven

Higher Power, as I understand you,
I pray to keep my connection with you open and clear from the confusion of daily life. Through my prayers and meditations, I ask especially for freedom from self-will, rationalization, and wishful thinking. I pray for the guidance of correct thought and positive action. Your will, Higher Power, not mine, be done.

(Taken from *Prayers for The Twelve Steps—A Spiritual Journey*, page 28)

Steps Ten and Eleven are the tools that help us trust God more fully and sustain the progress we have made in Steps One through Nine. In the first three steps, we recognized the seriousness of our condition and established the foundation for dealing with our problems. In Steps Four through Nine, we experienced a process similar to that of taking our car to the garage for a long-overdue, major overhaul. We devoted the time and energy required to make the necessary repairs and restore our "engine" to its proper running condition. In Steps Ten and Eleven, we have the opportunity to keep ourselves in tune by devoting time to regular service and maintenance. As we continue in this direction, we learn to recognize problems, to correct them promptly, and to continually seek God's guidance. This enhances our ability to improve our new skills for living life to the fullest. If we provide the required maintenance, we will find that our lives will run smoothly.

Prior to Step Eleven, we made contact with God in Steps Three, Five, and Seven. In Step Three, we made a decision to turn our wills and our lives over to his care. In Step Five, we admitted our wrongs to him. In Step Seven, we humbly asked him to remove our shortcomings. And now in Step Eleven, we use prayer and meditation to improve our conscious contact with God and to become more sensitive and responsive to his guidance.

Through the progress we have made in working the steps, we are learning more about what we want to achieve in the program. To protect what we have learned, we must continually seek to know God's will for us. A daily regimen of prayer and meditation makes it clear that relief from pain of the past is just a day-to-day reprieve. We must relentlessly seek to know God's will for us and how we are to live our lives. Those of us who have experienced the hell and chaos caused by our willful acts realize that we worshiped false gods such as drugs, sex, money, or addictive relationships. Surrendering to the Twelve-Step process was not the step that led us to heaven, but was, in fact, the step that led us out of the hell that our lives had become.

Spiritual growth and development occur slowly and only through discipline and reliance upon God. The best example of the discipline of prayer is that of Jesus as he prayed frequently to know his Father's will. In the Lord's Prayer, the singularly most important petition is "Thy will be done, on earth as it is in heaven." This might be interpreted as "May your will be realized throughout all of space, time, and creation. God, if it is to be done, it is for you to bring it about." As our self-esteem increases and our Higher Power becomes a trusted friend, we grow more confident that he is ever present with us when we pray. And we grow more confident that his will is what we want for our lives.

Meditation is an important way of seeking God's will for us, of setting aside our own intentions, and of receiving God's guidance. Meditation on Scripture is our best way to know God's will. Other forms of meditating can quiet our minds and remove the barriers of our conscious thoughts. When properly done, this process will calm us emotionally and relax us physically. We will release the energy we normally expend keeping our emotions in high gear and our bodies tense with anxiety.

Our approach to Step Eleven will vary in intent and intensity—it shows our commitment to a prayerful life. If we are communicating with God, his joy will infuse our fellowship and friendship with others. We will reap rich benefits. Ideally, we should practice this step throughout the day. The Apostle Paul encouraged believers to "pray without ceasing." But until we reach that goal, we should practice Step Eleven upon awakening and retiring. This discipline at the beginning and end of each day reminds us that we sincerely want god's will for our lives.

NOTE: Before proceeding, refer to **Guidelines for Prayer and Meditation** on page 198.

LOOKING TO SCRIPTURE

Praying only for knowledge of God's will for us and the power to carry it out helps us set aside our self-serving motives and interact well with others. We receive the reassurance of God's presence and the knowledge that his will is for us to be restored to health. Scripture gives examples of how we might behave when we allow God's will to work through us. In Luke 6:35–38, we are told: *"Love your enemies, do good to them, and lend to them...be merciful...do not judge...do not condemn...forgive...give..."* When we follow Christ's teachings and observe God's will for our lives, we experience peace and serenity.

> **"The good man brings good things out of the good stored up in his heart... For out of the outflow of his heart his mouth speaks."**   LUKE 6:45
>
> • • •
>
> *The goal of each of the steps is to improve our knowledge of God and our basic goodness and value as part of his creation.*

> **"Therefore I tell you, whatever you ask for in prayer, believe that you have received it, and it will be yours. And when you stand praying, if you hold anything against anyone, forgive him, so that your Father in heaven may forgive you your sins."**
>   MARK 11:24
>
> • • •
>
> *Our belief in God and the use of prayer are the principal tools that enable the Twelve Steps to support our recovery.*

Spending time in meditation enables us to become better acquainted with God in the same way that we become acquainted with someone we would really like to know. Meditation can be difficult at first. We are accustomed to being active and may feel uncomfortable with sitting still and calming our busy thoughts. We may feel we are wasting time, instead of doing something productive. Actually, nothing could be more productive.

> *"Let us acknowledge the Lord; let us press on to acknowledge him. As surely as the sun rises, he will appear; he will come to us like the winter rains, like the spring rains that water the earth."*
>
> HOS. 6:3
>
> • • •
>
> *Any difficulties we have in allowing God to come into our lives will be minimized as we acknowledge his presence throughout each day.*

Helpful Hint: Read Meditation for Hosea 6:3, page 144, *Meditations for The Twelve Steps—A Spiritual Journey.*

In the act of meditating, we ponder and apply our knowledge of God's ways. It is contemplation done in the presence of and with the help of God. It is two-way communion with him. In meditation, or "listening prayer," God makes himself known to us as we read scripture, reflect upon our lives, and contemplate God's deeds. Meditation's purpose is to clear our mental and spiritual vision and to let God's truth make its full and proper impact on our minds and hearts. Meditation humbles us as we contemplate God's greatness and glory and allow his Spirit to encourage, reassure, and comfort us.

"But when you pray, go into your room, close the door and pray to your Father, who is unseen. Then your Father, who sees what is done in secret, will reward you."   MATT. 6:6

. . .

Meditation may be new to us and feelings of discomfort may arise. With practice, we will realize the value of spending quiet time in contemplation and prayer. Once we learn a technique that is comfortable to us, we will never turn away.

"Show me your ways, O Lord, teach me your paths; guide me in your truth and teach me, for you are God my Savior, and my hope is in you all day long."   PS. 25:4–5

. . .

Being attentive to God's guidance requires our being conscious of the unexpected gifts that come to us each day. Giving thanks for all our opportunities to serve him heightens our sensitivity to the infinite way in which our Lord is leading us.

In developing a routine for prayer and meditation, we seek times and places to invite God's presence. Our desire is to be available for him. Some simple guidelines for learning to pray and meditate are:

• Pray, meditate, and study Scripture in solitude. Be alone and undisturbed, so you can be totally free from distractions.

• Pray and meditate in a peaceful environment, or talk quietly to God without interruptions. Outside influences disrupt your concentration and inhibit your ability to tell God your thoughts and feelings.

- Set aside quality time. Do not wait until you are tired.

- Listen carefully. God has messages for you, just as you have messages for him.

- Review your daily inventory with God. Admit your wrongs and make amends to him as needed.

- End your session by asking for knowledge of God's will for you and the power to carry it out.

> *"Ask and it will be given to you; seek and you will find; knock and the door will be opened to you."* MATT. 7:7
>
> • • •
>
> *Seeking to know his will and having the courage to carry it out are what our Lord has repeatedly instructed us to petition.*

If we are progressing satisfactorily with Step Eleven we will see signs along the way. We will feel more at peace in our daily affairs. We will experience deep gratitude for our ongoing healing. We will feel as though we have finally achieved a rightful place in the world. Feelings of self-worth will replace feelings of shame. These signs tell us that God is guiding and sustaining our recovery.

> *"on his law he meditates day and night. He is like a tree planted by streams of water, which yields its fruit in season and whose leaf does not wither."*
> PS. 1:1–3
>
> • • •
>
> *If we walk in the way of the Lord, the fruits of the Spirit will appear, much as the fruits of our physical world appear in nature.*

When we combine prayer and meditation with self-examination, we discover the secret to successfully working the steps. We find an effective means for maintaining a rewarding spiritual life. No matter how dedicated we are to recovery, we all have moments of doubt about the direction of our lives. We may even question the need to continue working the steps. Sometimes, we are tempted to regress to our old compulsive behavior. We tend to be especially vulnerable when we feel pressured for accomplishment or when we expect events to follow our own time schedule. In our frustration, we seize control from God's hands and attempt to hasten the process through our own willfulness. When we do this, we are not following God's guidance and must renew the commitment we made in Step Three.

> *"Your word is a lamp to my feet and a light for my path. I have taken an oath and confirmed it, that I will follow your righteous laws."*
>
> PS. 119:105–106
>
> • • •
>
> *We were stumbling in darkness, when through God's grace a lamp was lighted to show us the way. Our commitment is to follow the light.*

Helpful Hint: Read "Peace in God's Will," page 39, *Prayers for The Twelve Steps—A Spiritual Journey.*

Our power to carry out God's will can be challenged in those moments when our lives seem to be crumbling. The best example of faithfulness is found in Christ. He persevered during the challenges of his ministry, passion, and crucifixion. The strength of his faith can be summarized by the prayer he prayed in Gethsemane. He was overwhelmed by what lay before him: *"...My Father, if it is possible, may this cup be taken from me. Yet not as I will, but as you will."* (Matt. 26:39) During stressful moments, reflecting on Steps Three and Eleven can help us maintain our peace and serenity.

> *"Do not be anxious about anything, but in everything, by prayer and petition, with thanksgiving, present your requests to God."* PHIL. 4:6
>
> • • •
>
> *In the midst of anxious conflict, we can come to the Lord in prayer. He is able to give us serenity to accept the things we cannot change, courage to change the things we can, and wisdom to know the difference.*

Prayer and meditation give us an opportunity to seek God's plan for us. He gave us intellect and free will, through which we think and act. As part of practicing Step Eleven, we must not create excuses to delay our actions or rationalize that we are "waiting" for God's will. Part of doing God's will is taking action, trusting that God's Holy Spirit is working through us.

> *"If you believe, you will receive whatever you ask for in prayer."* MATT. 21:22
>
> • • •
>
> *Keeping a diary of how God answered our prayers through individuals or new experiences is one way to document our new life in Christ.*

Helpful Hint: Read Recovery Note for Matthew 21:18–22, *Life Recovery Bible.*

In unclear situations, it is sometimes wise to seek outside counsel. As God continues to reach out to us revelations may come to us through other people or new experiences. If the messages are unclear, we must be patient—more will be revealed to us. If we cannot wait, we should select the best course of action and trust that God is with us, guiding us as we go. Faith in him will allow us to receive what we need. The way we feel and function clearly shows if God's will is being done.

> *"But the one who hears my words and does not put them into practice is like a man who built a house on the ground without a foundation. The moment the torrent struck that house, it collapsed and its destruction was complete."*   LUKE 6:49
>
> • • •
>
> *Doubting God has consequences with which we are all too familiar. Perhaps our lack of faith caused the despair that led us to the Twelve-Step program of recovery.*

Our earthly walk with God is designed to bring us a life that is fulfilling. This is God's will for us as described in the teachings of Jesus. We can practice Jesus' teaching by praying the prayer he taught, "...your kingdom come, your will be done..." If we begin our day with that attitude of prayer, our daily lives will exemplify Step Eleven.

> *Whether you turn to the right or to the left, your ears will hear a voice behind you, saying, "This is the way; walk in it."*   ISA. 30:21
>
> • • •
>
> *The Holy Spirit responds to every prayer for help and guidance. His lesson for us is always unique to each situation.*

"PRAYER OF SAINT FRANCIS OF ASSISI"

Lord, make me an instrument of your peace!
Where there is hatred—let me sow love
Where there is injury—pardon
Where there is doubt—faith
Where there is despair—hope
Where there is darkness—light
Where there is sadness—joy
O Divine Master, grant that I may not so much seek
To be consoled—as to console
To be loved—as to love
for
It is in giving—that we receive
It is in pardoning—that we are pardoned
It is in dying—that
we are born to eternal life.
Amen.

KEY IDEAS

Prayer: Our Higher Power is more than an idea or a force. Our Higher Power is a person, Jesus Christ. Prayer is not merely an exercise in spiritual discipline. Prayer for us is conversation with a person who loves us very much. Prayer is the communication we need to maintain in a living relationship with our Savior. For help with prayer in its many forms, see *Prayers for The Twelve Steps—A Spiritual Journey*. It was written and compiled by Friends in Recovery to aid you in your spiritual journey.

Meditation: The word "meditation" implies various things to various people. Some seem frightened of meditation while others glorify it. But meditation itself is neither intrinsically good nor bad. It is a tool that is as effective or ineffective as the one using it. If practiced regularly, meditation will improve our relationship with God and increase our insight into Scripture.

Meditation must be approached spiritually. It is not an exercise for our minds, it is a practice for our spirits. Our overworked mental processes have sustained our distraction; our meditative practice will serve our spiritual needs. Meditation has often been called listening prayer because in meditation, we quiet our hearts and minds and open our spirits to God.

Conscious Contact: Communication with God is called many things. In the seventeenth century, a monk named Brother Lawrence coined the phrase "practicing the presence of God." The Apostle Paul referred to this communication as unceasing prayer. Step Eleven calls this prayerful communion "conscious contact with God." Whatever we call it, the idea is fellowship and connection with God. Prayer and meditation draw us into this relationship with God and enable us to understand his ways and his will.

God's Will: Every human being created by God has a will of his or her own. In the beginning that free will was used to rebel against God. The result was sin, disease, pain, death, and trouble of every kind. The only way to reverse the misery, which began in the Garden of Eden and bore fruit in us, is to choose God's will over our own. Step Eleven reminds us that the best prayer we can pray is for knowledge of God's will and the power to carry that out.

GUIDELINES FOR PRAYER
AND MEDITATION

The wisdom and guidance contained in God's word is available to us any time of the day or night. The principles of the Twelve Steps are woven throughout the Bible. Both God's word and the steps are useful tools for us wherever we are in our spiritual journey. An overview of prayer and meditation for a given day may be outlined as follows.

At the beginning of the day, review your plans and:

• Ask God for direction in your thoughts and actions.

  – To keep you free from self-pity, dishonesty, or selfishness.

  – To provide the guidance needed to take care of any problems.

• Ask God for freedom from self-will.

  – To prevent making requests unless others will be helped.

  – To avoid praying for our own selfish needs.

During the day, in moments of indecision or fear:

• Ask God for inspiration and guidance.

• Reflect on Step Three and turn it over.

  – Relax and breathe deeply several times.

  – Be aware of any desire to struggle with a situation or person.

• Pray to God as often as necessary during the day.

  – God, please remove this (feeling, obsession, addiction, etc.)

  – Lord, not my will, but thine be done.

• If possible, call a support person to identify and share what is happening.

At the end of the day, review the events that happened and:

- Reflect on Step Ten and take a personal inventory.
  - Ask God for guidance in taking corrective action.
- Ask God for knowledge of his will for you.
- Ask God's forgiveness where needed, and acknowledge that this review is not intended to cause obsessive thinking, worry, remorse, or morbid reflection.
- Give thanks to God for the guidance and blessings that were part of the day.

Helpful Hint: Read pages 151–155, *Prayers for The Twelve Steps—A Spiritual Journey*—On these pages the various types of prayer are concisely described and exemplified.

STEP TWELVE

Having had a spiritual awakening as the result of these Steps, we tried to carry this message to others, and to practice these principles in all our affairs.

. . .

Brothers, if someone is caught in a sin, you who are spiritual should restore him gently. But watch yourself, or you also may be tempted.

(GAL. 6:1)

Understanding Step Twelve

In most every house with children there is a certain wall or a doorpost with pencil marks. These pencil marks, which have dates or ages next to them, keep track of growth. Every few months the kids back up against the wall while mom or dad mark their height. Sometimes the growth is barely noticeable and other times the growth is drastic.

Step Twelve is a time for noticing growth. Through God's grace and our commitment to work the steps, we have had a life-changing spiritual experience. We began this journey as frightened tyrants desperately clinging to control our own little kingdoms. But we end this round of our journey with a new king on the throne: God. We experienced a rebellion that we led against ourselves. With God's help, we removed our kingdom and established God's. Although we know we have grown through this process, the mark on the wall is a little shorter—it's minus the crown.

Working Step Twelve

Step Twelve involves taking time to appreciate the spiritual growth in our lives. We work this step by sharing the program with others and continuing to practice the principles of the steps in every area of our lives.

Preparing for Step Twelve

We can prepare for Step Twelve by ensuring that God has been a part of every aspect of our program. If we have merely added God as an ingredient to our recovery, we will not notice any spiritual awakening in Step Twelve. If we have maintained control throughout the steps and worked them with rigorous zeal, we will find no spiritual awakening now. However, the spiritual awakening of Step Twelve will be ours if we have done all of the following: relied upon God's presence, worked the steps in partnership with him, and given him control of our will and lives.

Prayer for Step Twelve

Dear God,

My spiritual awakening continues to unfold. The help I have received I shall pass on and give to others, both in and out of the fellowship. For this opportunity I am grateful.

I pray most humbly to continue walking day by day on the road of spiritual progress. I pray for the inner strength and wisdom to practice the principles of this way of life in all I do and say. I need You, my friends, and the program every hour of every day. This is a better way to live.

(Taken from *Prayers for The Twelve Steps—A Spiritual Journey,* page 30)

The Twelfth Step completes the climb of this particular mountain. Remembering the milestones during this adventure reminds us of the pain and joy we experienced while accomplishing our objective. Our experiences have been unique and personal to each of us. We now realize that all the events of our lives have pulled together to show us our connection to God. Our spiritual awakening has changed us, so now we have the capacity to live our lives as an expression of God's will. An example of this type of transformation is beautifully captured in Titus 3:3–7:

> *"At one time we too were foolish, disobedient, deceived and enslaved by all kinds of passions and pleasures. We lived in malice and envy, being hated and hating one another. But when the kindness and love of God our Savior appeared, he saved us, not because of righteous things we had done, but because of his mercy. He saved us through the washing of rebirth and renewal by the Holy Spirit, whom he poured out on us generously through Jesus Christ our Savior, so that, having been justified by his grace, we might become heirs having the hope of eternal life."*

Step Twelve states that share God's message of hope and healing with others. Many of us were introduced to this Program by someone who was working Step Twelve. Now we have the opportunity to promote our own growth by helping others. We look for ways to demonstrate our new confidence because of our commitment to recovery and our growing awareness of God's presence in our lives. This program calls us to live our program daily and testify to the effectiveness of the Twelve Step principles. The Apostle Peter instructed us in this action by saying: *"But in your hearts set apart Christ as Lord. Always be prepared to give an answer to everyone who asks you to give the reason for the hope that you have. But do this with gentleness and respect..."* (1 Pet. 3:10)

This step reminds us that we have not yet completed our journey to wholeness. To continue our process of growth, we need to be aware that we have just begun to learn the principles that will enhance our walk with the Lord. Each of the Twelve Steps is a vital part of fulfilling God's plan for us. When our daily challenges distract and separate us from God, we can use the steps as tools for coping with our problems and drawing us back to God. **Step One reminds us of our powerlessness. Steps Two and Three show us the ongoing need for God's help. Steps Four through Nine guide us through self-examination and amends making. Steps Ten and Eleven help us minimize our slips and keep us in touch with God.** We are blessed through our conscientious attention to seeking God's will and to working the steps. Our blessings may include a level of love, acceptance, honesty, selflessness, and peace of mind that we never experienced before. The hardest part of any journey is the beginning, and this step is our milestone. **By reaching Step Twelve, we have shown our total commitment to God's will in our recovery.**

Our spiritual awakening is a gift that instills in us a new perspective. It is usually accompanied by a positive and significant change in our value system. Our pursuit of worldly goals has been subdued and redirected. We now look for fulfillment from things with real and lasting value. For most of us, the awakening is subtle and best seen in hindsight. It seldom has a distinct beginning and ending. We also realize it took all of this to get us here—that's why we were asleep for so long. As we awaken to the presence of God's love for us, our lives become filled with new purpose and meaning. In Romans 13:11, Paul tells us: *"The hour has come for you to wake up from your slumber, because our salvation is nearer now than when we first believed."*

LOOKING TO SCRIPTURE

"Actions speak louder than words" is an accurate description of how we should carry the Twelve-Step message to others. It is more effective to witness a principle being applied than to hear lectures on theory alone. For example, sharing our own experiences of prayer and meditation has more meaning than simply lecturing and explaining why everyone should meditate and pray. Telling our story will help others recognize their need for a relationship with God and encourage the growth of our own humility. When we tell our story, honesty and transparency are important. Others relate best when we are open about our lives.

Carrying the message gives us an opportunity to describe the ways in which God's Spirit works through the Twelve Steps to transform our lives. Each day our life experiences remind us how we are renewed in our relationship with God, our Higher Power. Through our sharing, we can convey the message of our experience, strength, and hope.

> *Finally, brothers, whatever is true, whatever is noble, whatever is right, whatever is pure, whatever is lovely, whatever is admirable—if anything is excellent or praiseworthy—think about such things. Whatever you have learned or received or heard from me, or seen in me—put it into practice. And the God of peace will be with you.* PHIL. 4:8–9
>
> • • •
>
> *We must take action on what we know to be true. Our actions speak for us and are a clear measure of our commitment to demonstrate God's love in our lives.*

Helpful Hint: Read "Prayers of Praise," Chapter Eleven, pages 137–145, *Prayers for The Twelve Steps—A Spiritual Journey.*

Scripture contains dramatic examples of the results of personal testimony about God's interaction in human affairs. John 4:28 and John 9:17 are accounts of personal experiences with Jesus Christ and their impact on the lives of others. Those who knew the speakers were convinced of the power of Christ's presence by the changes they witnessed.

> *Be wise in the way you act toward outsiders; make the most of every opportunity. Let your conversation be always full of grace, seasoned with salt, so that you may know how to answer everyone.*
>
> COL. 4:5–6
>
> • • •
>
> *The Twelve Steps are instruments that God uses to communicate the message of Christ's healing love. When asked, God tells us how we can best convey his message to others. We must listen and act as we are led.*

We cannot separate Twelve-Step work from our Christian walk; they are connected by our Lord's guiding hand. The action segment of Step Twelve is perfectly described in Romans 10:10: *"For it is with your heart that you believe and are justified, and it is with your mouth that you confess and are saved."*

> *Jesus did not let him, but said, "Go home to your family and tell them how much the Lord has done for you, and how he has had mercy on you."*
>
> MARK 5:19
>
> • • •
>
> *Jesus Christ constantly praised God for his good gifts. He urges us to pray to our Heavenly Father without ceasing.*

Working with newcomers to the program can be very rewarding. Many of them are troubled, confused, and resentful. They need guidance and help to understand that God will strengthen and change them through their Twelve-Step work. Through their willingness and commitment, they will experience rewards and miracles that far outweigh their present pain. We can encourage newcomers to work the program one day at a time. This can be a growth experience for us. As we reflect on where we were when first introduced to the program, we see how far we have come. When carrying the message, we can emphasize an important point about our decision to join the program. We made the decision only after we suffered enough, were discouraged, were tired of hurting, and had "hit bottom."

Preach the word; be prepared in season and out of season; correct, rebuke and encourage—with great patience and careful instruction. 2 TIM. 4:2

• • •

Sharing the story of our healing and recovery is the testimony God wants others to hear. Each of us has a unique pilgrimage to relate, and someone will receive encouragement from our message.

Helpful Hint: Read Recovery Note for 2 Timothy 4:1–5, *Life Recovery Bible.*

Be imitators of God...and live a life of love, just as Christ loved... EPH. 5:1–2

• • •

To keep the fire of our spiritual awakening alive, Step Twelve also requires that we practice the principles in all our affairs, giving away the love we have received.

Our relationship with God is the key to our success in everything, particularly in working the steps and applying the principles to our daily affairs. We cannot allow ourselves to drift into indifference and neglect our commitment to living according to the teachings of Christ. Scripture reminds us of the mandate to live a Christlike life. Scripture also tells us how we will know if we fail: *"No one who lives in him keeps on sinning. No one who continues to sin has either seen him or known him"* (1 John 3:6). Life constantly reminds us that we need to be prepared to face temptations and trials. But, with God's help, we can transform them into occasions for growth and comfort to ourselves and to those around us. We will never achieve peace and serenity independently of God's grace and Holy Spirit.

> *If anyone speaks, he should do it as one speaking the very words of God. If anyone serves, he should do it with the strength God provides, so that in all things God may be praised through Jesus Christ. To him be the glory and the power forever and ever. Amen.*　　　1 PET. 4:11
>
> • • •
>
> *Through the power of the Holy Spirit, we will receive the strength to be instruments of God's healing in the world.*

Sometimes we become discouraged and lose sight of our progress. If this happens, we compare our past to our present and ask ourselves:

• Are we less isolated and no longer afraid of people in authority?

• Have we stopped seeking approval from others and accepted ourselves as we really are?

- Are we more selective of the people with whom we develop relationships, and more able to keep our own identity while in a relationship?
- Have we developed the ability to express our feelings?
- Have we stopped trying to dominate others?
- Are we no longer behaving childishly by turning friends or spouses into protective parents and being too dependent?
- Have we become attentive to the needs of our inner child?

Affirmative answers show the extent of our progress toward a healthier and better way of living.

> *Brother, if someone is caught in a sin, you who are spiritual should restore him gently. But watch yourself, or you also may be tempted.* GAL. 6:1
>
> • • •
>
> *Because of our own struggle, we can in some way relate to the conflict others may be encountering. Being candid and compassionate in conveying the Twelve-Step message may assist others in making the commitment to turn their lives over to Jesus Christ.*

Helpful Hint: Read Meditation for Galatians 6:1, page 164, *Meditations for The Twelve Steps—A Spiritual Journey.*

An important achievement in working the steps occurs when we become accustomed to "living" the steps. We do this by habitually taking a problem or concern through the steps, while acknowledging our need for God's support and guidance. The result is peace and serenity and a new confidence that we can deal directly with the problems.

Any action we take is then guided by God's will and our honest appraisal of the consequences. We can act confidently and without fear, affirming *"The Lord is my light and my salvation—whom shall I fear? The Lord is the stronghold of my life—of whom shall I be afraid?"* (Psalm 27:1)

> ***Two are better than one, because they have a good return for their work: If one falls down, his friend can help him up. But pity the man who falls and has no one to help him up! Also, if two lie down together, they will keep warm. But how can one keep warm alone?*** ECCLES. 4:9–11
>
> • • •
>
> *The power of God's presence is increased when two or more are gathered in his name. Helping each other to know the way and keep the faith is central to the work of Step Twelve.*

At this point, we begin to identify the many areas of our lives that are being affected by working the Twelve Steps. Our success with handling new problems is linked to our willingness to thoughtfully take action, while remembering to let go and turn it over to God. Our faith grows as we learn to relinquish control and allow God to be the director of our lives.

The process is gradual, regenerative, and neverending. We slowly become more God-centered as we learn the true meaning of God's love, our surrender, and spiritual serenity. Paul captured the heart of this Twelve-Step process when he said: *"Brothers, I do not consider myself yet to have taken hold of it. But one thing I do: Forgetting what is behind and straining toward what is ahead, I press on toward the goal to win the prize for which God has called me heavenward in Christ Jesus"* (Phil. 3:13–14).

"No one lights a lamp and hides it in a jar or puts it under a bed. Instead, he puts it on a stand, so that those who come in can see the light. For there is nothing hidden that will not be...brought out into the open. Therefore consider carefully how you listen. LUKE 8:16–18

• • •

The Lord spreads his message through the Twelve Steps, and we are instruments for delivering it. The daily practice of these principles will confirm to others the sincerity of our commitments.

Each new day is a gift from God that we can accept and acknowledge joyfully as an answer to our prayer for serenity.

"SERENITY PRAYER"

God, grant me the serenity
to accept the things I cannot change,
the courage to change the things I can,
and the wisdom to know the difference.
Living one day at a time,
enjoying one moment at a time;
accepting hardship as a pathway to peace;
taking, as Jesus did,
this sinful world as it is,
not as I would have it;
trusting that You will make all things right
if I surrender to your will;
so that I may be reasonably happy in this life
and supremely happy with You
forever in the next. Amen
Reinhold Niebuhr

KEY IDEAS

Spiritual Awakening: The spiritual awakening that Step Twelve speaks of is a gradual change in the control of our lives. This change eventually produces a realization that we sincerely trust God and can depend on him. We also realize that this new trust and dependence brings a peace and serenity that we have never experienced before. We come to Step Twelve with confidence that God can be trusted, miracles do happen, and prayer works.

Carrying the Message: In Step Twelve we are encouraged to carry the message of the Twelve Steps to others. If we have read the *The Big Book of Alcoholics Anonymous*, we realize that early program members always understood that they were carrying a spiritual message. The message we carry is that God can save us from our sin, from our self-defeating behavior, from our despair, from our torment—God can save us from ourselves. We carry a spiritual message that only God is able to control our lives and heal us. We will live more productive and healthy lives if we yield to a power greater than ourselves.

TWELVE-STEP REVIEW

Identify a situation or condition in your life that is currently a source of resentment, fear, sadness, or anger. It may involve relationships (family, work, or sexual), work environment, health or self-esteem. Write a concise statement describing the situation and identify your concern.

Use the following exercise to apply the principles of the Twelve Steps to the above.

Step One: Describe the ways in which you are powerless in this situation. How does this situation show you the unmanageability of your life?

Step Two: In what ways do you need your Higher Power to restore you to sanity?

Step Three: Write an affirmation in which you state your decision to turn this situation over to God. (e.g., I am no longer willing to fret over my boss's behavior. I decide now to turn my anxiety, my concerns, and my need for security over to God.)

Step Four: What character defects have surfaced (e.g., fear of abandonment or authority figures, control, approval seeking, obsessive/compulsive behavior, rescuing, excessive responsibility, unexpressed feelings)?

Step Five: Admit your wrongs to God, to yourself, and to another.

Step Six: Reflect upon your willingness to have God remove the character defects that have surfaced. Describe your willingness or reasons for not being willing.

Step Seven: Write a prayer in which you humbly ask God to remove the specific shortcomings relating to this situation. (You can be most humble when you are honest about your shortcomings and your needs.)

Step Eight: Make a list of the persons who have been harmed.

Step Nine: Describe how you intend to make the necessary amends.

Step Ten: Review the above steps to be sure that nothing has been overlooked. Consider whether this process has brought up anything new for you to work on.

Step Eleven: Take a moment for prayer or meditation, asking God for knowledge of his will for you. What is your understanding of God's will in this situation?

Step Twelve: In this situation have you come to sense a spiritual awakening? Who is in charge now, you or God? Explain. (Your attitude and emotions are good indicators.)

APPENDIX ONE

MEETING FORMAT

Leader:

"Hello, and welcome to **The Twelve Steps for Christians** support group meeting. My name is _____ and I am your trusted servant for today's meeting. Please join me for a moment of silence, after which we will recite the Serenity Prayer."

"SERENITY PRAYER"

God, grant me the serenity
to accept the things I cannot change,
the courage to change the things I can,
and the wisdom to know the difference.
Living one day at a time,
enjoying one moment at a time,
accepting hardship as a pathway to peace;
taking, as Jesus did, this sinful world as it is,
not as I would have it;
trusting that You will make all things right
if I surrender to your will;
so that I may be reasonably happy in this life
and supremely happy with You
forever in the next. Amen.

Reinhold Niebuhr

"We are a support group committed to creating a safe place for men and women to share their experience, strength, and hope with each other."

"As a fellowship of men and women recovering from behaviors that have affected us in our lives, our purpose is to grow spiritually and in our relationship with God. For our guide, we use the Bible and *The Twelve Steps for Christians* to help us on our journey of recovery. We are here for our own benefit, to share our own experience, strength and hope with others. We are not here to talk about others, to condemn, criticize, or judge them. Our desire is to improve the quality of our lives as we apply what we learn from listening to and sharing with each other. Our hope is in the belief that we can succeed today in situations where we failed previously. As we place ourselves in the care of our Higher Power, Jesus Christ, our attitudes improve as we honestly, openly, and willingly look at who we are and engage in healthier behavior."

"I've asked _____ to read **The Twelve Steps**."

"I've asked _____ to read the **Scripture for the Twelve Steps** after each step."

"Many of the principles and traditions of Alcoholics Anonymous are used as part of the basis of our group. We respect the confidentiality and anonymity of each person here. Remember that whatever you hear at this meeting is shared with the trust and confidence that it will remain here. Who you see here, what is said here, when you leave here, let it stay here."

"We are self-supporting through our own contributions. We ask for your contribution at this time." (Take time for collection before continuing.)

"If you are new to a Twelve-Step support group, we offer you a special welcome and invite you to attend at least 6 meetings to give yourself a fair chance to decide if this group is for you. We encourage you to exchange phone numbers with other members for support between meetings. Phone lists, literature, and information on other recovery support groups will be available after the meeting. If you have any questions, please feel free to talk with me at the end of the meeting."

"Is there anyone here today for the first time? If so, please tell us your first name so we can greet you."

"We will now introduce ourselves by first name only. My name is _____."

"This meeting is a step study using *The Twelve Steps for Christians.* The Twelve Steps represent a spiritual discipline that can provide a way out of destructive behavior and an opportunity to improve our relationship with our Higher Power, Jesus Christ."

"Everyone is invited to share, but no one is obligated to do so."

"Today's meeting focuses on Step _____. We will read a portion of the chapter, after which we will begin our time of sharing. Please turn to page _____."

"Please keep your sharing focused on recent experiences and events. Focus on your personal experience, strength, and hope."

"Limit your sharing to 3 to 5 minutes. Allow everyone in the group to share once before you share a second time."

"Please...*no cross talk.* Cross talk occurs when individuals speak out of turn and interrupt one another. The group is disrupted, and focus is diverted from the individual whose turn it is to speak."

(NOTE TO FACILITATOR: 10 minutes before closing ask for prayer requests.)

"We will now take time for prayer requests. These requests should be regarding yourself or other group members."

Closing:

"This is a fellowship of (church or organization name) and is intended to complement other Christ-centered Twelve-Step groups. You are encouraged to attend other Twelve-Step recovery support groups during the week to support your recovery journey."

"I've asked _____ to read the **Milestones in Recovery.**" (Page 219)

"Are there any announcements?"

"Reminder! What you hear at this meeting is confidential; leave it at this meeting! It is not for public disclosure or gossip. Please respect the privacy of those who have shared here today."

"Will everyone please clean up after themselves and help rearrange the room?"

"Will all who care to, stand and join me in closing with the Lord's Prayer?"

"KEEP COMING BACK, IT WORKS!"

NOTES TO FACILITATOR

• *Appendix One* contains review questions for writing or sharing on this step.

• Leader begins the sharing by telling his or her story as it pertains to the step being discussed. Allow per person a maximum of 10 minutes to share.

• If the group is larger than 20 people it is advisable to form small groups of 5 to 7 people for the sharing portion of the meeting.

MILESTONES IN RECOVERY

Through God's help and our work in the Twelve-Step program, we can look forward to achieving the following milestones in recovery.

- We feel comfortable with people, including authority figures.
- We have a strong identity and generally approve of ourselves.
- We accept and use personal criticism in a positive way.
- As we face our own life situation, we find we are attracted by strengths and understand the weaknesses in our relationships with other people.
- We are recovering through loving and focusing on ourselves; we accept responsibility for our own thoughts and actions.
- We feel comfortable standing up for ourselves when it is appropriate.
- We are enjoying peace and serenity, trusting that God is guiding our recovery.
- We love people who love and take care of themselves.
- We are free to feel and express our feelings even when they cause us pain.
- We have a healthy sense of self-esteem.
- We are developing new skills that allow us to initiate and complete ideas and projects.
- We take prudent action by first considering alternative behaviors and possible consequences.
- We rely more and more on God as our Higher Power.

QUESTIONS FOR STEP REVIEW

Step One

We admitted we were powerless over the effects
of our separation from God, that our lives
had become unmanageable.

Step One forms the foundation for working the other steps. Admitting our powerlessness and accepting the unmanageability of our lives is not an easy thing to do. Although our behavior has caused us stress and pain, it is difficult to let go and trust that our lives can work out well. The idea that there are areas over which we are powerless is a new concept for us. It is much easier for us to feel that we have power and are in control.

. . .

In what area of your life do you experience the strongest need to be in control?

What are the consequences of your self-destructive habits?

What difficulties are you having in recognizing your powerlessness and your life's unmanageability?

What major event in your life has caused you to realize the extent of your pain?

Step Two

Came to believe that a power greater than
ourselves could restore us to sanity.

Step Two gives us new hope to see that help is available
to us if we simply reach out and accept what our Higher
Power, Jesus Christ, has to offer. It is here that we form
the foundation for growth of our spiritual life, which helps
us become the person we want to be. What is required of
us is a willingness to believe that a power greater than
ourselves is waiting to be our personal Savior. What follows
as we proceed through the steps is a process that brings
Jesus Christ into our lives and enables us to grow in love,
health, and grace.

• • •

List experiences that caused you to lose faith in God.

Have you mistakenly believed that it was your responsibility
to create faith yourself instead of accepting faith as a gift?
Explain.

What is keeping you from truly believing that a power greater
than yourself can restore you to sanity?

Describe your inability to manage your own affairs.

Step Three

Made a decision to turn our will and our lives over
to the care of God *as we understood Him.*

Step Three is an affirmative step. It is time to make a
decision. In the first two steps, we became aware of our
condition and accepted the idea of a power greater than
ourselves. Although we are beginning to know and trust
God, we may find it difficult to think of allowing him to
be totally in charge of our lives. However, if the alternative
is facing the loss of something critical to our existence,
God's guidance may be easier to accept.

• • •

Which parts of your life are you willing to turn over to
God?

Which parts of your life are you unwilling to turn over to
God? What prevents you from giving them up?

Why do you suppose that surrendering your life to God
reduces the stress in your life?

What do you hope to experience as a result of your decision
to surrender to God's will?

Step Four

Made a searching and fearless
moral inventory of ourselves.

Step Four is a tool to help us understand our current behavior patterns and recognize our need for God's guidance in our lives. Here, we examine our behavior and expand our understanding of ourselves. Being totally thorough and honest in preparing our inventory helps us to see the obstacles that have prevented us from knowing ourselves and acknowledging our deepest feelings about life.

• • •

What is your major strength? How does it support you?

What is your major weakness? How does it hurt you?

Which of your present behaviors is the most damaging to your life? Explain.

In what areas of your life do you suspect that denial is at work?

Step Five

Admitted to God, to ourselves, and to another human
being the exact nature of our wrongs.

Step Five requires that we engage in honest confrontations
with ourselves and others by admitting our faults to God,
to ourselves, and to another person. By doing so, we begin
to set aside our pride and see ourselves in true perspective.
We also realize how our growing relationship with God
gives us the courage to examine ourselves, accept who we
are, and reveal our true selves. Step Five helps us acknowledge and discard our old survival skills and move toward
a new and healthier life.

• • •

What can be gained by admitting your faults to another
person?

What is your resistance to sharing your story with another
person?

Which of your faults is the most difficult to acknowledge?
Why?

In what ways will admitting to God, to yourself, and to
another stop you from deceiving yourself?

Step Six

Were entirely ready to have God remove
all these defects of character.

The task of removing our ineffective behavior is more
than we can handle alone. Step Six does not indicate that
we do the removing; all we have to do is be "entirely ready"
for it to happen. We can become ready by faithfully working
the steps and being willing to let God assist us in removing
our shortcomings. The character traits we want to eliminate
are often deeply ingrained patterns of behavior. They will
not vanish overnight. We must be patient while God is
shaping us into new people. Allowing God be in control
helps us to trust him more completely.

• • •

What do you fear by having your character defects removed?

Identify two character defects you are not ready to have
removed.

Why is it necessary to learn humility before God can remove
your defects of character?

What is interfering with your readiness to have God remove
your shortcomings?

Step Seven

Humbly asked Him to remove our shortcomings.

Humility is the central idea of Step Seven. By practicing humility we receive the strength necessary to work the steps and achieve satisfactory results. We recognize that a major portion of our lives has been devoted to fulfilling our self-centered desires. We must set aside these prideful, selfish behavior patterns and realize that humility frees our spirit. Step Seven requires surrendering our will to God so that we may receive the serenity necessary to achieve the happiness we seek.

. . .

How are you benefiting from God's presence in your life?

What special blessings has God sent to you since you began your Twelve-Step program of recovery?

List examples that indicate you are practicing humility.

Which of your negative character traits are becoming positive? Explain how this change is impacting your life.

Step Eight

Made a list of all persons we had harmed, and became willing to make amends to them all.

Step Eight begins the process of healing damaged relationships through our willingness to make amends for past misdeeds. We prepare ourselves to carry out God's master plan for our lives by preparing to make amends. We can let go of our resentments and start to overcome the guilt, the shame, and low self-esteem we have acquired through our harmful actions. Through the gift of the Twelve Steps, we have the necessary tools to overcome these damaging conditions and mend our broken friendships.

• • •

List three personal experiences that require making amends.

How will making amends help free you from resentment and shame?

How does your unwillingness to forgive others block your progress and hurt your relationship with God?

Why is forgiving yourself an important factor in the amends-making process?

Step Nine

Made direct amends to such people wherever possible, except when to do so would injure them or others.

Step Nine fulfills our requirement to reconcile with others. We clear our "garden" of dead leaves and "rake up and discard" the old habits. We face our faults, admit our wrongs, and ask for and extend forgiveness. Making amends will release us from many of the resentments of our past. It is a means of achieving serenity in our lives by seeking forgiveness from those we have harmed and making restitution where necessary.

• • •

How will completing Step Nine enable you to bury the past and improve your self-esteem?

What difficulties are you having in making amends?

Who on your amends list causes you the most anxiety? What is the cause of this anxiety?

Who on your amends list do you consider to be an enemy? How do you plan to make this amend?

Step Ten

Continued to take personal inventory and, when we
were wrong, promptly admitted it.

Step Ten points the way toward continued spiritual
growth. We consciously examine our daily conduct and make
adjustments where necessary. We look at ourselves, see our
errors, promptly admit them, and make corrections. Taking
regular inventory makes us more conscious of our strengths
and weaknesses. We are less inclined to yield to feelings
of loneliness, self-righteousness, and anger if we remain
emotionally balanced and gather courage as we see our
strengths increasing. We become more focused and capable
of living the Christian life we desire.

• • •

List an example that shows you are relating better to others.

Cite a recent situation in which you did not behave appropriately. What did you do when you realized you were
in error?

How does taking a daily inventory support your spiritual
growth?

How does correcting your wrongs save you from unnecessary
consequences?

Step Eleven

Sought through prayer and meditation to improve our
conscious contact with God *as we understood Him,*
praying only for knowledge of His will for us
and the power to carry that out.

To protect what we have learned, we must continually
seek to know God's will for us. A daily regimen of prayer
and meditation makes it clear that relief is just a day-to-day
reprieve. Our approach to Step Eleven will vary in intent
and intensity; it indicates our commitment to a prayerful
life. If we are communing and are communicating with
God, his joy will infuse our fellowship and friendship with
others. We will reap rich benefits. Ideally, we practice this
step daily upon awakening and retiring, to remind us that
we must sincerely and humbly want God's will for us.

• • •

Describe a situation where you delayed taking action because
you were "waiting" for God's will. What happened?

Cite an example in which God answered your prayers
through another individual or a new experience.

What do you experience when quietly praying to God?

How has your life improved as a result of working the
steps?

Step Twelve

Having had a spiritual awakening as the result of these
steps, we tried to carry this message to others, and
to practice these principles in all our affairs.

Each of the Twelve Steps is a vital part of fulfilling God's
plan for us. Conscientious attention to working the steps
develops in us a level of love, acceptance, honesty, and
peace of mind unequalled at any other time in our lives.
Step Twelve invites us to promote our own growth by helping
others. Our willingness to share our commitment to recovery
and our growing awareness of God's presence in our lives
keep us ever-vigilant for ways to share our new confidence.

• • •

Cite an example that shows you are "living" the steps.

List a concern you had and describe your experience of
resolving it by applying the Twelve Steps.

What connection do you see between the Twelve Steps and
your Christian walk?

How do you practice the principles of the steps in all your
affairs?

APPENDIX TWO

We invite you to visit our current internet website at www. rpipublishing.com.

RPI Publishing, Inc. was founded on the belief that people in recovery need support from one another. It can't be done alone, we need the help of others. It is for this reason that we encourage you to find people who understand and can share with you in the recovery journey. We recommend that you contact the organizations listed on "Hot Links" at our website to help you in your search for information, support and understanding.

We at RPI Publishing, Inc. believe strongly in the power of the Twelve Steps and the guidance they provide to help rebuild a person's life. We founded the company on the principles of Step Twelve which states, "Having had a spiritual awakening as the results of these steps, we tried to carry this message to others and to practice these principles in all our affairs."

Our mission is to "carry the message to others" who are healing from the traumas of their past. Our website displays titles which include books on spirituality, personal growth, and self-help. Central to our message of faith, hope and recovery is that spiritual growth in the basis for all healing through God's Grace, for those who seek God's help, through Jesus Christ, to rebuild their lives.

We acknowledge that recovery is a lifetime process of change and growth. As we've learned more about recovery, we've become increasingly aware of the many issues that can affect us physically, emotionally, and spiritually.

We appreciate the continued support of our friends on the journey of restoration and recovery through a renewed relationship with God, ourselves and others.

A portion of the proceeds from the sale of our publications goes to support recovery work.

RPI Publishing, Inc. – PO Box 44 – Curtis, WA 98538
(800) 873-8384 – Fax (360) 245-3757
Internet address: http://www.rpipublishing.com

APPENDIX THREE

SELF-HELP RESOURCES

Christian Group Resources

Alcoholics for Christ
(800) 441-7877

Alcoholics Victorious
(800) 624-5156
Website: http://www.iugm.org/av/

Christian Help Lines Inc.
(813) 874-5509

Christian Recovery Connection
http://crc.iugm.org/
The Christian Recovery Connection is a "virtual community" where believers can share their experience, strength and hope and access helpful resources that support spiritual growth and healing.

Christian Recovery International
(714) 529-6227
C.R.I. affiliated ministries that help the Christian community become a safe place for people recovering from addictions, abuse or trauma.
National Association for Christian Recovery
http://www.christianrecovery.com/nacr.htm
Clergy Recovery Network
http://www.christianrecovery.com/graceworks.shtml

Tools for Recovery
http://www.christianrecovery.com/twelvestep.shtml
Vencedores
http://www.christianrecovery.com/vencedores.shtml

Confident Kids Support Groups
(805) 473-7945
Website: http://www.christianrecovery.com/cktop.htm

Overcomers Outreach Inc.
National Network of support groups.
(714) 491-3000
Email: info@oo.sheperd.com

Overcomers
(402) 571-6837

The Florida Net
c/o Ron Ross
(407) 269-6702
Email: TheNet@digital.net

Secular Groups – National Hotlines

CHILD ABUSE
National Family Violence Hotline (800)222-2000

DOMESTIC VIOLENCE
National Domestic Violence Hotline (800) 799-7233

DRUGS & ALCOHOL
Nat'l Council on Alcoholism and Drug Dependence
(800) 622-2255
Teen Help Adolescent Resources (800) 637-0701
National Substance Abuse Hotline (800) DRUG-HELP

GAMBLING
Nat'l Council on Compulsive Gambling (800) 522-4700

Secular Support Group Networks

ALCOHOL & DRUGS
Adult Children of Alcoholics
(310) 534-1815
Internet: http://www.lafn.org/community/aca

Alcoholics Anonymous World Services
(212) 870-3400
Internet: http://www.alcoholics-anonymous.org

Al-Anon Family Groups
(757) 563-1600
Internet: http://www.al-anon.org

Alateen
(800) 344-2666
Internet: http://www.alateen.org

Co-Anon Family Groups
(714) 647-6698

Cocaine Anonymous
(800) 347-8998 (24 hr)
Internet: http://www.ca.org

Narcotics Anonymous
(818) 773-9999
Internet: http://www.wsoinc.com

CODEPENDENCY
Co-Dependents Anonymous
For U.S. group info call (602) 277-7991
Internet: http://www.ourcoda.org

DOMESTIC VIOLENCE
Batterers Anonymous
(909) 355-1100
Email: jmgoff@genesisnetwork.net

EATING DISORDERS
National Eating Disorders Organization
(918) 481-4044
http://www.laureate.com

Overeaters Anonymous
(505) 891-2664
Internet: http://www.overeatersanonymous.org

GAMBLING
Gamblers Anonymous
(213)386-8789
http://www.gamblersanonymous.org

Gam-Anon Family Groups
(718) 352-1671 (Tues. and Thurs., 9am-5pm)

SEXUAL ABUSE
VOICES In Action, Inc.
(773) 327-1500 or (800) 7-VOICE-8
http://www.voices-action.org

Incest Survivors Resource Network Int'l
(505) 521-4260
http://www.zianet.com/ISRNI

SEX ADDICTION
Augustine Fellowship, Sex and Love Addicts Anonymous
(617) 332-1845

S-Anon
(615) 833-3152
http://www.sanon.org

COSA (Codependents of Sex Addicts)
(612) 537-6904

Sexaholics Anonymous
(615) 331-6230
http://www.sa.org

Sex Addicts Anonymous
(713) 869-4902

WORK ADDICTION
Workaholics Anonymous
(510) 273-9253